KALLIS' iBT TOEFL® PATTERN

Writing 1

TOEFL® is a registered trademark of Educational Testing Services (ETS), Princeton, New Jersey, USA. The content in this text, including the practice prompts, Model Answers, and Hacking Strategies, is created and designed exclusively by KALLIS. This publication is not endorsed or approved by ETS.

KALLIS' iBT TOEFL® Pattern Writing 1

KALLIS EDU, INC.
7490 Opportunity Road, Suite 203
San Diego, CA 92111
(858) 277-8600
info@kallisedu.com
www.kallisedu.com

Copyright © 2014 KALLIS EDU, INC.

All rights reserved. No part of this book may be reproduced, stored in a retrieval system, or transmitted in any form or by any means, electronic or mechanical, including photocopying, recording, or otherwise, without the prior written permission of the copyright owner.

ISBN-10: 1-4996-1319-9
ISBN-13: 978-1-4996-1319-3

iBT TOEFL® Pattern - Writing I is the first of our three-level iBT TOEFL® Writing Exam preparation book series.

Our **iBT TOEFL® Pattern Writing** series simplifies each TOEFL writing task into a series of simple steps, ensuring that students do not become overwhelmed as they develop their writing skills. Our commitment to minimizing instruction and maximizing student practice provides students with many opportunities to strengthen their writing skills while developing a unique writing style.

KALLIS

KALLIS'

TOEFL® iBT
PATTERN
WRITING 1
BASIC SKILLS

Getting Started

A study guide should familiarize the reader with the material found on the test, present unique methods for solving various question types, and provide practice questions to challenge future test-takers. *KALLIS' iBT TOEFL® Pattern Series* aims to accomplish all these study tasks by presenting iBT TOEFL® test material in an organized, comprehensive, and easy-to-understand way.

KALLIS' iBT TOEFL® Pattern Writing Series provides in-depth explanations and practices to help you prepare for the iBT TOEFL writing section. Each writing task is broken down into a series of steps, allowing you to develop reliable and efficient writing strategies.

Developing Basic Skills

Chapter 1 is devoted to developing the basic grammar, vocabulary, and writing skills necessary for composing clear and effective iBT TOEFL writing responses. This chapter consists of explanatory sections, which introduce new grammar and writing skills, and practices that allow you to develop these skills.

Understanding the Writing Tasks

The beginning of Chapters 2 and 3 provide introductory information that is designed to familiarize you with the two types of writing tasks encountered in the iBT TOEFL writing section. These sections will prepare you for the subsequent explanations and practices.

General Information

The **General Information** section presents the writing skills that you will need to complete the writing portion of the iBT TOEFL and provides descriptions of each writing task.

Response Format

The **Response Format** section provides an outline that explains how to organize your writing task responses. This section provides general information regarding how many paragraphs a response should consist of, as well as what information should be included in each paragraph.

Hacking Strategy

The **Hacking Strategy** provides a step-by-step process outlining how to organize and compose writing task responses. Each step that is outlined in the **Hacking Strategy** section is elaborated on in detail throughout the chapter.

Improving Writing Skills through Practice

A combination of explanations and practices breaks down each writing task into simple step-by-step processes.

Practices

In Chapters 1, 2, and 3, each section that contains grammar- or essay-composition information is followed by one or more *Practices*. These provide opportunities to develop the skills that you just read about. Each *Practice* builds upon information presented earlier in the chapter, allowing you to gradually develop skills that you will use when you are writing your responses.

Exercises

Exercises require you to use skills developed in each chapter to complete a writing task response. Each *Exercise* provides a series of outline and writing templates designed to help you organize and compose your response. An Integrated Writing task *Exercise* is located at the end of Chapter 2, and an Independent Writing task *Exercise* is located at the end of Chapter 3.

Actual Practice

Chapter 4 consists of four *Actual Practices*, which provide templates to help you outline and compose Integrated and Independent writing responses. Thus, *Actual Practices* require you to use skills from all Practices, so *Actual Practices* should only be attempted after you are familiar with the structure of the iBT TOEFL writing section.

Actual Test

The *Actual Test* section, which is located in Chapter 5, presents an Integrated prompt and an Independent prompt in a format that resembles the official iBT TOEFL writing test. Because this section does not contain the detailed templates given in the *Exercises* or the Actual Practices, this section should be attempted only after all writing skills have been mastered.

In Case You Need Help

▶ Toward the back of this book, you will find the **Answer Key**, which provides model answers to the **Practices** from Chapters 1, 2, and 3. Model answers are also included immediately after their corresponding **Exercises** and **Actual Practices/Test**.

▶ These model answers demonstrate one acceptable way to answer each question, but there will often be many acceptable responses. So do not feel that your responses must be the same as the model answers, just use them for guidance when necessary.

Table of Contents

Chapter 1

GRAMMAR SKILLS

SKILL 1 ♦ The Basics
A.	Simple Sentence Structures	2
B.	Generalized Nouns	4
C.	Articles	6
D.	Determiners	8

SKILL 2 ♦ Verbs
A.	Action and Linking Verbs	10
B.	The Present Tense	12
C.	The Future and Past Tenses	14
D.	The Present and Past Perfect Tenses	16
E.	Active and Passive Voice	18
F.	Causative Verbs	20

SKILL 3 ♦ Pronouns
A.	Personal Pronouns	22
B.	Relative and Demonstrative Pronouns	24
C.	Indefinite Pronouns and Pronoun Agreement	26

SKILL 4 ♦ Improving Clarity
A.	Degrees of Comparison	28
B.	Gerunds and Infinitives	30
C.	Gerunds and Infinitives as Objects	32
D.	Improving Vocabulary	34
E.	Improving Language	36
F.	Sounding Formal	38
G.	Phrases	40

SKILL 5 ♦ Multi-part Sentences
A.	Clauses	42
B.	Conjunctions	42
C.	Compound and Complex Sentences	44
D.	Transitions	46

Chapter 2

PRACTICING INTEGRATED WRITING

SKILL 1 ♦ General Information
A.	The Integrated Writing Task	50
B.	Integrated Writing Format	51
C.	Hacking Strategy – Integrated	52

SKILL 2 ♦ General Writing Skills
A.	Taking Notes	53
B.	Connecting Information	56
C.	Reporting Verbs and Phrases	58
D.	Citing Information	58

SKILL 3 ♦ Integrated Essay Organization
A.	The Introduction	62
B.	The Body Paragraphs	64

Exercise & Model Answer   66

SKILL 4 ♦ Integrated Essay Checklist
A.	Proofreading and Editing	74

WRITING 1

BASIC SKILLS

Chapter 3

PRACTICING INDEPENDENT WRITING

SKILL 1 ♦ General Information
A. The Independent Writing Task 78
B. Independent Response Format 79
C. Hacking Strategy – Independent 80
D. Independent Question Types 81

SKILL 2 ♦ Necessary Information
A. Creating a Personal Profile 84
B. Creating a Timeline 86

SKILL 3 ♦ Introduction
A. Introduction Format 88
B. Brainstorming Ideas 88
C. General Statement 94
D. Thesis 95

SKILL 4 ♦ The Body Paragraphs and Conclusion
A. Including Explanations 102
B. The Conclusion 106

Exercise & Model Answer 108

SKILL 5 ♦ Independent Essay Checklist
A. Proofreading and Editing 112

Chapter 4

ACTUAL PRACTICE

Actual Practice 1 118
Actual Practice 2 126
Actual Practice 3 134
Actual Practice 4 142

Chapter 5

ACTUAL TEST 152

Appendix

ANSWER KEY 162

Before You Begin...

INTEGRATED AND INDEPENDENT TASKS

The iBT TOEFL Writing test consists of two tasks: one Integrated task and one Independent task.

The first task is called the "Integrated task" because it requires you to incorporate, or integrate, material from spoken and/or written sources into your response. This task will require you to read a passage, listen to a lecture, and then form a response based on what you have read and heard.

The second task is called the "Independent task" because it requires you to produce a response without using any extra written or spoken materials. Thus, you must come up with responses to the second task independently, using your own experiences or opinions.

TRANSITION WORDS AND PHRASES

Transition words and phrases explain how the content of one sentence relates to the rest of your response.

Meaning	Examples
addition	*additionally, furthermore, in addition, in fact, moreover*
cause-and-effect	*as a result, consequently, therefore, to this end*
compare/contrast	*compared to, despite, however, in contrast, on the contrary, on the one hand, on the other hand, nevertheless*
conclusions	*finally, in conclusion, in summary, lastly, thus, in short*
examples	*for example, for instance, in this case, in this situation*
introductions	*according to, as indicated in/by, based on*
reasons	*one reason is, another reason is, due to*
sequence	*afterward, again, finally, first, next, previously, second, third*

SYMBOLS AND ABBREVIATIONS

When taking notes to prepare for a written response, save time by using symbols and abbreviations instead of complete words. You can create your own symbols and abbreviations in addition to using those listed in the charts on the following page.

Symbol	Meaning	Symbol	Meaning
&	and	=	equals, is
%	percent	>	more than
#	number	<	less than
@	at	→	resulting in
↓	decreasing	↑	increasing

ABBREVIATIONS FOR UNIVERSITY ACTIVITIES

Abbreviation	Meaning	Abbreviation	Meaning
edu.	education	RA	resident assistant
GE	general education	stu.	student
GPA	grade point average	TA	teaching assistant
prof.	professor/professional	univ.	university

ABBREVIATIONS FOR ACADEMIC TOPICS

Abbreviation	Meaning	Abbreviation	Meaning
bio.	biology/biological	exp.	experience/experiment
c.	century	info.	information
chem.	chemistry/chemical	gov.	government
def.	definition	hypo.	hypothesis
econ.	economics/economy	phys.	physics/physical
env.	environment	psych.	psychology/psychological
ex.	example	sci.	science/scientific

OTHER ABBREVIATIONS

Abbreviation	Meaning	Abbreviation	Meaning
abt.	about	pic.	picture
b/c	because	ppl.	people
comm.	community/communication	pref.	preference
e/o	each other	pt.	point
fam.	family	ques.	question
fav.	favorite	s/b	somebody
gen.	general/generation	s/o	someone
hr.	hour	sec.	second
impt.	important	w/	with
loc.	location	w/i	within
lvl.	level	w/o	without
min.	minute	yr.	year

TOEFL PATTERN WRITING 1

Chapter 1

GRAMMAR SKILLS

THE BASICS

A. SIMPLE SENTENCE STRUCTURES

Although writing tests are not grammar tests, using grammar correctly when writing an essay is important. Above all, remember that a sentence must express a complete thought.

When writing a sentence, remember to capitalize the first letter and to use proper punctuation at the end. Also, remember that every sentence must have a subject and a verb. Of course, sentences may also contain many other parts.

1. **SUBJECT**
   The *subject* is the person or thing that performs the action or experiences the condition described in the sentence. The subject can be a *noun, pronoun, noun phrase, noun clause, infinitive verb,* or *gerund*.

2. **VERB**
   A *verb* usually tells what the subject of the sentence is doing. *Action verbs* show the action of the subject, and *linking verbs* show state of being.

3. **OBJECT**
   An *object* is the noun affected by the subject of the sentence. There are two types of objects: *indirect objects* and *direct objects*.

4. **MODIFIER**
   A modifier describes or modifies another part of speech. A *modifier* that describes a noun is called an **adjective**; a *modifier* that describes a verb or another adjective is an **adverb**.

5. **COMPLEMENT**
   A *complement* is a noun, a pronoun, or an adjective that follows a subject or an object and gives essential information about the subject or object.

I. **Subject + Verb (Action)**
   The lecturer disagrees. / The airplane flies.

II. **Subject + Verb (Linking) + Adjective (Subject Complement)**
   Surgery may be necessary. / The evidence seems weak.

III. **Subject + Verb + Object**
   I received the news. / The passage provides information.

IV. **Subject + Verb + Indirect Object + Direct Object**
   He built his daughter a dollhouse. / The child told his parents the truth.

V. **Subject + Verb + Object + Object Complement**
   We painted the house blue. / The police caught the boy stealing.

PRACTICE 1 Rewrite the scrambled words and phrases so that they form complete sentences. Be sure to capitalize the first letter and put a period (.) at the end of each sentence.

1) his elders / respects / a leader

   → *A leader respects his elders.*

2) correct / seems / the statement

   → _____

3) did / many experiments / the researcher

   → _____

4) with their families / celebrate / many people / holidays

   → _____

5) many months / on her research project / spent / the student

   → _____

6) journalists / the facts / present / to readers

   → _____

PRACTICE 2 Determine which of the following are complete sentences and which are sentence fragments. Write "S" if the phrase is a complete sentence, and "F" if it is a fragment.

1) __F__ Not according to the study.
2) __S__ Many people visit the museum.
3) _____ Because it is more ancient.
4) _____ Molecules in the air.
5) _____ Books can teach us nearly everything.
6) _____ The future is unknown to humans.
7) _____ The city is always exciting.
8) _____ Yet, also a little bit tiring.
9) _____ To educate more of the country's population.
10) _____ In the past, plastic was not available.

PRACTICE 3 Add words to the following sentence fragments to create complete sentences.

1) An important day of the year _____.

2) My home country _____.

GRAMMAR SKILLS ♦ CHAPTER 1

B. GENERALIZED NOUNS

1. COUNTABLE NOUN

A *countable noun* is a noun that can easily be counted. For example, you can count how many fingers you have on your hands, so "finger" is a countable noun. Countable nouns can be either singular or plural.

> **Ex** woman, chair, star, plate, table, mountain, country
> → *women, chairs, stars, plates, tables, mountains, countries*

2. UNCOUNTABLE NOUN

An *uncountable noun* is something that cannot be divided into individual pieces, so it cannot be counted. Generally, uncountable nouns have no plural form.

> **Ex** sand, hunger, housework, money, water, furniture, equipment

When making general statements in English, plural nouns are often preferable to singular nouns. Make countable nouns plural when they refer to people, places, things, or ideas that are not proper nouns.

> **Ex** A student should try to follow a direction when taking a test.
> → Better: **Students** should try to follow **directions** when taking **tests**.

> **Ex** A person should always help another who is in need.
> → Better: **People** should always help **others** who are in need.

Change the following unnatural-sounding sentences into natural-sounding sentences by making singular nouns plural when doing so is appropriate.

1) Many people like to celebrate a winter holiday.
   → *Many people like to celebrate winter holidays.*

2) A holiday is a great time to visit a friend.
   → _____

3) During the winter, it is easy for a person to spread an illness to another person.
   → _____

4) A sick person should stay home to avoid spreading a germ.
   → _____

5) A parent enjoys playing a video game with his or her child.
   → _____

Rewrite the following sentences, replacing all underlined nouns and pronouns with their plural forms. Then change the underlined verbs to match the nouns they refer to.

1) The <u>lesson</u> in her <u>class was</u> good because a <u>student</u> could understand <u>it</u>.

   → *The **lessons** in her **classes were** good because **students** could understand **them**.*

2) The lecture disputes the claim that <u>a computer</u> will completely replace <u>a human</u> in <u>a workplace</u>.

   →

3) <u>A person</u> often <u>relies</u> on the support of <u>a family member</u> during <u>a difficult time</u>.

   →

4) Reading <u>a newspaper article</u> and watching <u>a news program</u> can help <u>a person</u> stay informed about <u>a current event</u>.

   →

5) <u>A small country</u> may require <u>a young person</u> to serve as <u>a soldier</u>, which may provide <u>him</u> or <u>her</u> with <u>a valuable life experience</u>.

   →

6) <u>A child</u> who <u>excels</u> in <u>a sport</u> may receive <u>a college scholarship</u>, or <u>he or she</u> may even receive <u>an offer</u> from <u>a professional sports team</u>.

   →

7) <u>A firefighter</u> must be willing to place <u>himself or herself</u> in <u>a dangerous situation</u>, such as entering <u>a burning building</u> or putting out <u>a forest fire</u>.

   →

8) <u>A cellular phone</u> that can access the Internet <u>is</u> the best <u>gift</u> that <u>a parent</u> can give to <u>his or her child</u> because <u>a cellular phone provides</u> access to useful information.

   →

C. ARTICLES

An article functions much like an adjective, as both modify nouns. The two articles in English are *the* and *a/an*. The lack of an article before a noun is called the *zero article*.

Place an article before the noun it modifies, and if an adjective modifies the same noun, place the article before the adjective as well, such as in the noun phrase "a hot pan."

1. THE DEFINITE ARTICLE

▶ The only definite article in English is the word *the*. Place *the* before nouns that refer to a particular member of a group. In other words, *the* refers to specific nouns.

▶ *The* can be used with singular and plural countable nouns as well as uncountable nouns.

2. THE INDEFINITE ARTICLE

▶ The indefinite articles used in English are *a* and *an*. Indefinite articles indicate that a noun is non-specific and does not refer to a particular member of a group. In the statement, "I would like *a* dog," the speaker is not requesting a particular dog, just expressing a desire for any dog.

▶ "*A/An*" can be used with singular countable nouns or be included in the phrase *a _____ of* + uncountable noun (*a grain of* sand, *a blade of* grass, *a strand of* hair).

▶ **When to use "a" versus when to use "an"**

- *a* + singular noun beginning with a consonant or consonant sound: a cat, a university
    * "university" begins with a vowel, but the "u" makes a consonant "yoo"/"ju" sound.
- *an* + singular noun beginning with a vowel: an elephant, an orange, an umbrella
- *an* + singular noun beginning with a silent "h": an hour, an honor, an heir

3. ZERO ARTICLE

▶ The following categories of nouns do NOT require an article:

- names of nationalities and languages: Italian, German, Korean
- names of sports: football, basketball, tae-kwon do
- names of academic subjects: mathematics, physics, literature
- names of people: Mark, Hector, Sarah
- uncountable nouns that refer to general things or concepts: sugar, loyalty, honesty

PRACTICE 1 — The following sentences are missing articles. Fill in the appropriate *article* for each blank spot.

1) __The__ Empire State Building is one of __the__ tallest buildings in __the__ world.

2) _____ sperm whale can hold its breath for over _____ hour.

3) I received _____ trophy in _____ talent show's awards ceremony.

4) _____ Los Angeles earthquake caused wall decorations to fall to _____ floor.

5) While hiking, Dillon saw _____ eagle glide down and capture _____ mouse.

6) _____ process of photosynthesis gives plants _____ energy that they need to survive.

7) _____ Himalaya mountain range contains _____ tallest mountain on Earth.

PRACTICE 2 — The following sentences are missing *articles*. Rewrite each sentence with the appropriate articles. In some cases, both an indefinite and definite article may be correct.

1) Hannah took dog for walk around block.

   → *Hannah took the dog for a walk around the block.*

2) Final exam was so easy that it only took students hour to finish.

   → _____

3) Elephant at zoo is largest animal that I have ever seen in person.

   → _____

4) In year 1969, Neil Armstrong became first man to walk on Moon.

   → _____

5) One leg of table was shorter than other legs, so Sam put wedge under it.

   → _____

6) While at beach, I ate sandwich and watched waves crash into sand.

   → _____

7) Octopus was able to escape its aquarium by squeezing its body through crack in aquarium lid.

   → _____

D. DETERMINERS

Articles fall under a broad category of words called **determiners**, which introduce noun phrases and tell the reader whether noun phrases contain specific or general information.

Some determiners pair with countable nouns while others pair with uncountable nouns. Therefore, you must memorize which determiners pair with which type of noun.

1. DETERMINERS THAT PAIR WITH PLURAL COUNTABLE NOUNS

many (of)	(a) few	several	a couple of
a number of	the number of	both	numerous

Many people went home before the rock concert ended.
A few audience members stayed until the end of the long performance.

2. DETERMINERS THAT PAIR WITH UNCOUNTABLE NOUNS

(a) little	an amount of	amounts of	much (of)

Jack thought that there was not *much* sugar left in the jar.
However, he found *a little* sugar at the bottom of the container.

3. DETERMINERS THAT CAN PAIR WITH COUNTABLE OR UNCOUNTABLE NOUNS

all (of)	some	most (of)
any (of)	a lot of	plenty of

Countable Noun → *All of* the children finished their dinners.
Uncountable Noun → After dinner, the children drank *all of* the milk.

When you want to compare or contrast two related groups, use the formation "Some… while others…."

Some whales possess teeth *while others* have baleen, which they use to filter out their food from the ocean water.

When you want to compare or contrast three related individuals or groups, use the formation "One group…; another (group)…; the other(s)…."

One circus performer was able to swallow a sword; *another* was able to walk on a tightrope; *the other* was able to ride a unicycle.

PRACTICE 1

The following sentences contain determiner-related errors. Fix the errors by rewriting each sentence.

1) There is many coffee left.

   → *There is plenty of coffee left.*

2) Much of the students failed their tests.

   →_____

3) Many flour is needed for the cake recipe.

   →_____

4) I cannot believe that little of my friends want to see a movie.

   →_____

5) Some people like to wake up early while another people like to sleep in.

   →_____

PRACTICE 2

Complete the rewrite of each phrase by using an appropriate *determiner* from the following word bank.

> a little   a couple of   some
> most of   several   plenty of

1) about three times

   Rephrase → _____*several*_____ times

2) two mistakes

   Rephrase → _____ mistakes

3) a small amount of tea

   Rephrase → _____ tea

4) a large amount of work

   Rephrase → _____ work

5) the majority of the apples

   Rephrase → _____ the apples

6) less than half of the water

   Rephrase → _____ water

SKILL 2 VERBS

A. ACTION AND LINKING VERBS

Verbs have various tenses, which are formed by using or adding to a verb's base form. The **base form** of a verb is the most basic spelling of a verb. Knowing the base form is useful because it allows you to determine what kind of spelling changes the verb may undergo.

1. ACTION VERB

An action verb expresses *what the subject does.*
run, jump, spin, cheat, type, reach, explode

- **Subject + Action Verb**

  I walk. / It began.

- **Subject + Action Verb + Object**

  Peter studies philosophy. / The ball hit the ground.

- **Subject + Action Verb + Adverb**

  The car spins uncontrollably. / The lecturer speaks softly.

2. LINKING VERB

A linking verb connects the subject to information that describes the subject.
Typical linking verbs include:
be, become, seem, remain, feel, appear, look

- **Subject + Linking Verb + Adjective**

  The theory is correct. / Flying to the moon seemed impossible.

- **Subject + Linking Verb + Noun**

  The twins are artists.
  The Rub' al Khali is one of the largest deserts in the world.

▶ **The linking verb "be"** has many different forms that must be memorized.

	I	You	He/She/It	We	They
Past Tense	was	were	was	were	were
Present Tense	am	are	is	are	are
Future Tense	will be	will be	will be	will be	will be

PRACTICE 1

Use the subject in parentheses and the appropriate verb from the word bank to complete the sentences.

> sing   collect   dive   attach
> is   rely   eat   make

1) Out of all the animals that have ever lived on Earth, ___*the blue whale is*___ the biggest. (the blue whale)

2) _____ hundreds of tons of small shrimp during summer. (blue whales)

3) _____ hundreds of meters underwater to prey on squid. (sperm whales)

4) _____ "tags" to whales so that they can track them by satellite. (researchers)

5) _____ on their hearing as much as humans depend on vision. (most whales)

6) _____ many noises, including whistles and moos. (Beluga whales)

7) _____ beautiful songs to attract a female. (a male humpback whale)

8) Underwater _____ data about where individual whales go. (microphones)

PRACTICE 2

Complete each sentence by filling in the correct form of the verb "*be*."

1) Just about everyone ___*is*___ thankful when receiving gifts.

2) I _____ always happy to get presents.

3) Holidays _____ often about spending time with loved ones.

4) In some ancient cultures, gifts _____ a way of sharing wealth.

5) I predict that gift-giving _____ popular far into the future.

B. THE PRESENT TENSE

Remember that a verb's *tense* shows when an action takes place. Therefore, the present tense describes current habits, routines, and conditions. Also use the present tense when describing what happens in a story or a film.

1. REGULAR PRESENT-TENSE FORMATION

The only tricky part of forming the present tense of regular verbs is remembering to add an "s" to the end of the verb when it is used with he, she, or it.

	Singular	Plural	Example
1st Person	I *exercise*	we *exercise*	I **exercise** every day, you **exercise** every other day, and he **exercises** every weekend.
2nd Person	you *exercise*	you all *exercise*	
3rd Person	he, she, it *exercises*	they *exercise*	

2. IRREGULAR PRESENT-TENSE FORMATION

When forming the present tense, the he/she/it forms of some verbs require spelling changes.

▸ When the base form of the verb ends in a *consonant followed by "y"*, replace the "y" with *"ies"* for the third-person singular.

Ex study, cry, try, fly, apply, deny

	Singular	Plural	Example
1st Person	I *study*	we *study*	I **study** every night before going to sleep, but my friend John never **studies**.
2nd Person	you *study*	you all *study*	
3rd Person	he, she, it *studies*	they *study*	

▸ Additionally, add *"es"* to verbs that normally end in *"o"* when forming the *third-person singular*.

Ex do, go, undergo, undo, forgo

	Singular	Plural	Example
1st Person	I *go*	we *go*	I **go** to college in California, but my brother **goes** to college in Washington.
2nd Person	you *study* you *go*	you all *go*	
3rd Person	he, she, it *goes*	they *go*	

PRACTICE 1 Fill in each blank space with the **third-person singular form** of the **present tense verb** in parentheses.

1) Each planet _____*takes*_____ a different amount of time to orbit the Sun. (take)

2) As a result, a solar year _____ longer on some planets than it does on others. (last)

3) Earth _____ its orbit around the Sun approximately once every 365 days. (complete)

4) However, Mercury _____ the Sun every 88 Earth days. (encircle)

5) Generally, a planet's orbit lengthens as its distance from the Sun _____. (increase)

PRACTICE 2 Fill in each blank space with the **third-person singular form** of the **present tense verb** in parentheses.

1) The student _____*goes*_____ to the cafeteria for every meal. (go)

2) My roommate always _____ homework in the library. (do)

3) The university often _____ requests for campus concerts. (deny)

4) Almost every night, she _____ until 11 p.m. (study)

5) When acting in the theater, my friend _____ easily. (cry)

6) The campus art gallery constantly _____ change. (undergo)

7) The professor often _____ for research grants. (apply)

8) The university _____ to offer enough of the popular classes. (try)

9) Sometimes my friend _____ parties in order to work. (forgo)

10) The class _____ research in the laboratory twice a week. (do)

11) The snack machine _____ all my efforts to eat healthily. (undo)

12) During school holidays, my friend always _____ home to Hawaii. (fly)

GRAMMAR SKILLS ♦ CHAPTER 1

C. THE FUTURE AND PAST TENSES

1. FUTURE TENSE VERBS

The future tense shows that an action or state of being has not happened yet but will in the future.

- **"Will" Formation**

    The base form of a verb with "will" refers to plans, predictions, and promises.
    Place the word "will" before the verb.

    > Ex I promise that I will study every night before I go to bed.
    >   If all goes well, Chung will compete in a marathon next year.

- **"Going to" Formation**

    The base form of a verb with "going to" refers to definite plans.
    Use the necessary form of "be" followed by "going" before the infinitive verb.

    > Ex The tests are going to change format next year.
    >   I am going to go to class in a few minutes.

2. PAST TENSE VERBS

The past tense shows that an action or state of being began and ended in the past.

- **Regular Formation**

    Add "ed" or "d" to the end of the verb.

    > Ex Martha work*ed* on her report all night long.
    >   Some students complete*d* the test faster than others.

- **Irregular Formation**

    There are hundreds of irregular English verbs. Some of the most common irregular past tense forms are listed below.

Present	Past	Present	Past
become	became	know	knew
begin	began	make	made
bring	brought	put	put
choose	chose	read	read
do	did	say	said
go	went	see	saw
fall	fell	speak	spoke
find	found	take	took
feel	felt	teach	taught
give	gave	come	came
have	had	think	thought
hear	heard	write	wrote

> Note If a verb's base form ends in "y," you must change the "y" to an "i" before adding "ed" to form the past tense. Thus, "try" becomes "tried."

Practice 1 Each sentence has two blank spots; fill one blank with a *past tense form* of the verb in parentheses, and fill the other blank with a *future tense form* of the same verb.

1) Yesterday they _____*worked*_____ on the experiment, and soon we _____*will work*_____ on it. (work)

2) Melissa _____ dinner for us last night, and she _____ dinner tonight as well. (prepare)

3) Although I _____ in the college dorms last year, I _____ in an apartment next year. (live)

4) Last week the instructor _____ about the context of the book, and today she _____ about its themes. (speak)

5) Earlier we _____ a grammar test, and later today we _____ a vocabulary test. (have)

6) He already _____ the notes on the website, and soon he _____ the slide show there as well. (put)

Practice 2 Fill in the blank space in each sentence with the *past tense form* of the verb.

1) John Adams, a colonial lawyer, _____*took*_____ part in planning the American Revolution in 1776. (take)

2) He supported the Americans, but he _____ British soldiers legal defense in court. (give)

3) It was Adams who _____ that George Washington would make a good leader. (see)

4) Adams _____ the case for the American side to invest in ships for its military. (make)

5) After the war, Adams _____ to France to make a peace treaty with Great Britain. (go)

6) Later, voters _____ him as the second president of the United States. (choose)

7) As president, Adams _____ that America needed a strong central government. (feel)

8) Adams also _____ that America should avoid involvement in European conflicts. (think)

9) Adams worked with Thomas Jefferson for many years and _____ him well. (know)

10) Adams _____ about the importance of balancing power in the new government. (speak)

11) John and Abigail Adam's son, John Quincy Adams, _____ the sixth president of the United States. (become)

D. PERFECTIVE AND PROGRESSIVE ASPECTS

Tense explains *when* something occurs, whereas **aspect** refers to how an event or action should be viewed with respect to time. In other words, aspects tells you whether an event or action is ongoing or completed. Tense and aspect are often combined when discussing conditions, changes, and narratives.

THE PERFECTIVE ASPECT

1. THE PRESENT PREFECT

The *present perfect* describes an action or state of being that happened in the past but affects present circumstances.

"have" or "has" + past participle form of verb

> **Ex** I **have** already **eaten** dinner.
>
> The theory **has explained** everything.
>
> Computers **have taken over** many jobs.

2. THE PAST PERFECT

The *past perfect* shows that an action or a condition continued until a specific time in the past.

"had" + past participle form of verb

> **Ex** I **had** always **expected** to be a farmer until I saw the city.
>
> Europeans **had** never **tasted** chocolate until they explored South America.
>
> The artist **had completed** many paintings by the time he died.

THE PROGRESSIVE ASPECT

The *progressive aspect* describes an action in progress at a point in the past, present, or future.

Appropriate form of "to be" + verb + ing

> **Ex** These days I **am thinking** about going to graduate school.
>
> Juliet **was dancing** at a party when Romeo first saw her.
>
> The researcher **was looking** over the data when he noticed an error.
>
> Humans **will be walking** on Mars someday.

PRACTICE 1 Change the verbs in parentheses to show *past* or *present progressive* or *perfect aspect*.

1) Even though I have _____*waited*_____ here for hours, I am _____*staying*_____ until a bus arrives. (wait, stay)

2) I have _____ what I was _____ about. (forget, talk)

3) By the time we had _____ a mile, the sky was _____ dark. (walk, become)

4) The spaceship is _____ because it has _____ power. (malfunction, lose)

5) Jesse has _____ all summer, which is why his team is _____ the game. (practice, win)

6) These students have _____ every test so far this year, and they are _____ for the final exam now. (pass, study)

PRACTICE 2 Answer the questions using your own ideas. Use the *present progressive* and the *present perfect*.

1) In your education, what are you planning to do? *Ex.: I am planning to attend a university.*

   → _____

2) In your education, what have you already done? *Ex.: I have completed high school.*

   → _____

3) Where are you planning to go for your next vacation? *Ex.: I am planning to go to Switzerland.*

   → _____

4) Describe a person you know who has quit something. *Ex.: My friend has quit his job as a waiter.*

   → _____

5) How is society changing? *Ex.: Society is becoming busier.*

   → _____

6) How has society changed during your lifetime? *Ex. More people have started shopping online.*

   → _____

E. ACTIVE AND PASSIVE VOICE

A verb's *voice* describes the relationship between an action or a state of being and the individuals affected by that action.

1. ACTIVE VOICE

When forming the *active voice*, the subject comes before the action it is performing.

- **Subject + Verb + Object**

  Ricardo   ate   the pizza.
  Wendy   lit   the candle.

Any sentence in which the subject comes before the verb in a sentence is in the active voice.

2. PASSIVE VOICE

Some *passive-voice sentences* do not contain an identifiable subject (either because the subject is unknown or because the subject is obvious and does not need to be stated); other *passive-voice sentences* are formed by switching the placement of the subject and the object in the sentence.

Passive-voice sentences are formed by placing an appropriate form of the verb "be" before the verb. But be careful: not every sentence containing a form of "be" is passive.

- **Object + Form of "be" + Verb + (Subject)**

  The cat   was   found   (by Greg).
  Andrew   was   tackled   (by Drew).

PASSIVE VOICE → ACTIVE VOICE

One of the main goals in academic writing is conveying ideas as clearly as possible. Because the *active voice* tells you who performs the action of a sentence, it conveys ideas clearly and is usually preferable in academic writing. Write using the active voice whenever possible.

To change passive sentences into active sentences:

1) locate the subject (determine who or what performs the action)
2) place the subject before the verb
3) place the object at the end of the sentence

- **PASSIVE VOICE SENTENCES**
  Johnny was fought by Jack.
  The wallet was lost by Tony.
  The toy was bought by Lisa.

- **ACTIVE VOICE SENTENCES**
  Jack fought Johnny.
  Tony lost his wallet.
  Lisa bought the toy.

PRACTICE 1 Change the following *passive-voice sentences* into *active-voice sentences*.

1) I was strongly influenced by my older sister.

   → *My older sister strongly influenced me.*

2) I was impressed by her hard work.

   → _____

3) Eventually, a job in the field of health care was chosen by her.

   → _____

4) Now, many people are helped by my sister when they get sick.

   → _____

5) I was taught by her the importance of having goals.

   → _____

PRACTICE 2 Change the following *passive-voice sentences* to *active-voice sentences* by using the appropriate subject from the word bank first and changing the verb to show the active voice.

| Grandma | The lost cat | Doctors | Gardeners |
| Psychologists | The writer | A loud noise | |

1) Tomatoes should be planted in spring.

   → ***Gardeners*** *should plant tomatoes in spring.*

2) A tree was climbed.

   → _____

3) The patient's life was saved.

   → _____

4) The deer was scared away.

   → _____

5) My homemade gift will be appreciated.

   → _____

6) A study was conducted to see why people like karaoke.

   → _____

7) Evidence is presented that proves his point.

   → _____

F. CAUSATIVE VERBS

Causative verbs show that the subject of a sentence is having someone else perform an action. Essentially, the subject causes something to happen without performing the action. The person performing the action is called the **agent**.

The most common causative verbs are *make*, *have*, *let*, *help*, and *get*.

Causative verbs are used in both active- and passive-voice sentences. See the charts below for the different ways to form causative sentences.

1. ACTIVE CAUSATIVE SENTENCE

FORMAT

Subject + Causative Verb + Agent + Base form of Verb + Object

Subject	Causative Verb	Agent	Base form of Verb	Object
Jim	made	Cody	wash	the car.
Annie	had	Lisa	cut	her hair.
Tristan	let	his son	eat	dessert.
Lorenzo	helps	Esteban	repair	the house.

2. PASSIVE CAUSATIVE SENTENCE

FORMAT

Subject + Causative Verb + Object + Past Participle

Subject	Causative Verb	Object	Past Participle
Annie	got	her hair	cut.
Cesar	had	his car	stolen.

 Very few causative verbs can be used as passive verbs. In formal English writing, "have" is the most common passive causative verb.

CAUSATIVE VERBS IN ACTION

Whenever it is logical, rewrite passive sentences as passive causative sentences, as they sound more natural in written and spoken English.

- PASSIVE VOICE
  Donna's toenails were painted.
  Sal's teeth were cleaned.
  Lee's radio was repaired.

- PASSIVE CAUSATIVE
  Donna had her toenails painted.
  Sal had his teeth cleaned.
  Lee had his radio repaired.

Practice 1 Rewrite the following *passive-voice sentences* as *active causative sentences*.

1) Fred's dog was made to go for a walk by Fred.

   → *Fred made his dog go for a walk.*

2) The tutor was made to explain the math problem by Ricky.

   → _____

3) The prisoners were let out of their cells by the guard.

   → _____

4) Martha's son was helped with his homework by Martha.

   → _____

5) The doctor was let by Caroline to look at her broken leg.

   → _____

6) Chelsea was helped by Richard when she moved her belongings.

   → _____

Practice 2 Rewrite the following *passive-voice sentences* as *passive causative sentences*.

1) Sammy's food order was taken.

   → *Sammy had his food order taken.*

2) Lisa's essay was corrected.

   → _____

3) Amy's clothes were cleaned.

   → _____

4) Doug's car was repainted.

   → _____

5) Joe's lost wallet was returned to him.

   → _____

6) Francis' dinner was delivered to his house.

   → _____

PRONOUNS

A. PERSONAL PRONOUNS

In order to make your English writing smoother and less repetitive, use pronouns to replace nouns that you have already mentioned in your writing. A **pronoun** is a word that substitutes a noun, noun phrase, or another pronoun but does not change the meaning of the sentence.

PRONOUNS AND CASE

A word's *case* shows how the word functions in a sentence. All nouns have case, but only pronouns change entirely when forming the three cases: nominative case, objective case, and possessive case.

- The *nominative case* of a pronoun is used when the pronoun is the **subject** of a sentence.
- The *objective case* is used when a pronoun is the **object** of a sentence or prepositional phrase.
- The *possessive case* is used when a pronoun is being used to show ownership.

Below is a list of personal pronouns that change form based on their case.

Person	Nominative Case	Objective Case	Possessive Case/ Possessive Pronoun
first-person singular	I	me	my/mine
first-person plural	we	us	our/ours
second-person singular	you	you	your/yours
second-person plural	you	you	your/yours
third-person singular	he, she, it	him, her, it	his/his, her/hers, its/(none)
third-person plural	they	them	their/theirs

Ex I always wear the bracelet that **my** best friend made for **me**.
Finding a new place to live is **your** responsibility.
The responsibility of finding a new home is **yours**.

Note When the possessive pronoun comes before the word it shows possession over, use the first possessive form in the table above. When the possessive pronoun comes after the word it shows possession over, use the second possessive form.

Practice 1 The following sentences are missing **pronouns**. Using the context of the sentence, fill in the proper pronouns in each sentence.

1) Daniel Day-Lewis is known for ___his___ acting skill and dedication.

2) Very few people can claim that _____ have been to every continent.

3) In the 19th century, Charles Darwin developed _____ theory of natural selection.

4) With _____ population nearing 1.4 billion people, China is the most populated country.

5) Skyler, Katie, and I decided that _____ will go on a road trip during _____ vacation.

6) The members of the band disagreed about where _____ should perform for _____ next show.

7) Many seabirds are monogamous, so when an albatross selects a mate, _____ stays with that mate for the rest of _____ life.

Practice 2 The following sentences contain pronouns with case-related errors. Rewrite each sentence by fixing pronoun errors.

1) Anthony took he dog for a walk.

   → *Anthony took his dog for a walk.*

2) The last piece of cake is your.

   → _____

3) The dog buried it bone in the yard.

   → _____

4) Help you brother with him homework.

   → _____

5) Mine mother told I to prepare dinner.

   → _____

6) The penguins returned to they nests with food.

   → _____

7) Sally and me walk to school with ours friends every day.

   → _____

GRAMMAR SKILLS ♦ CHAPTER 1

B. RELATIVE AND DEMONSTRATIVE PRONOUNS

1. RELATIVE PRONOUNS AND ADVERBS

A *relative pronoun/adverb* refers to the noun that came immediately before it in a sentence, and it is followed by a description of the noun being replaced.

Pronoun	What it refers to	Examples
who/whom	one or more people	Joyce, **who** runs the movie theater, is very kind.
which/that	one or more things	Gold, **which** is an element, is very valuable. The toy **that** I received for Christmas is broken!

Adverb	What it refers to	Examples
where	one or more places	The beach **where** I lost my umbrella is very windy.
when	a period of time	Christmas is a time **when** people give presents to each other.

2. DEMONSTRATIVE PRONOUNS

Demonstrative pronouns indicate, or point to, people, places, or things. They often refer to larger concepts or processes mentioned earlier in your writing.

Pronoun	When to use	Examples
this/that	To point out a single person, place, thing, or idea	Everyone today knows that the Earth is round, but scholars once debated **this** concept.
these/those	To point out multiple people, places, things, or ideas	**These** apples you picked taste delicious. Tickets for air travel are more expensive than **those** for rail travel.

 "This" and "these" refer to nouns that are physically close to the speaker while "that" and "those" refer to nouns that are physically far away from the speaker.

PRACTICE 1 Connect the two sentences by using *relative pronouns/adverbs* (*who*, *which/that*, *where*, or *when*). There may be more than one way to properly arrange each sentence.

1) I thanked the woman. + She helped me.

   → *I thanked the woman who helped me.*

2) Peter is very friendly. + He lives next door.

   → _____

3) The house is very old. + Julie lives in that house (there).

   → _____

4) Diana works in that office building. + It will be rebuilt soon.

   → _____

5) The hotel was not very clean. + We stayed in that hotel (there).

   → _____

6) Laurence's favorite fruit is kiwi. + It is the national fruit of China.

   → _____

7) Grandfather bought this property in 1934. + Land was very inexpensive at that time (then).

   → _____

8) California has very diverse geography. + California is the most populated state.

   → _____

PRACTICE 2 Complete the sentence by filling in each blank space with an appropriate demonstrative pronoun (*this*, *that*, *these*, or *those*). There may be more than one appropriate pronoun for an answer.

1) I found ____*these*____ old pictures while searching through the garage.

2) Do you want this umbrella or _____ one?

3) _____ two watches that I am holding are both broken.

4) I will retake the test, and _____ time I will study beforehand.

5) The salary of a top manager is much higher than _____ of a worker.

6) Warm, humid weather seems to be good for _____ types of flowers.

7) Classes at the university are more difficult than _____ at the community college.

8) The substances found in this lab are more dangerous than _____ found in the other lab.

GRAMMAR SKILLS ♦ CHAPTER 1

C. INDEFINITE PRONOUNS AND PRONOUN AGREEMENT

INDEFINITE PRONOUNS

An *indefinite pronoun* replaces a non-specific noun; the noun may be unspecified because it is obvious or because it is unknown. Unlike personal pronouns, indefinite pronouns do not necessarily have an *antecedent*, which is the word that a pronoun replaces within a sentence.

Singular Indefinite Pronouns	anyone, either, neither, no one, someone, one, each, other, nothing
Plural Indefinite Pronouns	both, several, few, many
Singular or Plural Indefinite Pronouns, depending on meaning	all, some, any, none

PRONOUN-ANTECEDENT AGREEMENT

A common error in English is referring to **SINGULAR** nouns or indefinite pronouns with **PLURAL** pronouns. Make sure that any pronouns agree in number with their antecedents. For instance, if a pronoun refers to a singular noun, make sure that the pronoun is also singular.

Ex

1) With today's technology, *anyone* can learn about *their* genetic background. X
→ With today's technology, *anyone* can learn about *his or her* genetic background. O

   Note As an alternative, change the indefinite pronoun to a plural noun:
→ With today's technology, *people* can learn about *their* genetic *backgrounds*. O

2) *A Siberian husky* is social and needs to be with others or *they* will try to escape. X
→ *Siberian huskies* are social and need to be with others or *they* will try to escape. O
→ *A Siberian husky* is social and needs to be with others or *it* will try to escape. O

3) *A student* should never be arrogant, even if *they* are the smartest person in *their* class. X
→ *Students* should never be arrogant, even if *they* are the smartest people in *their* classes. O
→ *A student* should never be arrogant, even if *he or she* is the smartest person in *his or her* class. O

Practice 1: The following sentences are incorrect. Rewrite each sentence so the *indefinite pronouns* agree with all pronouns, nouns, and verbs in the sentence.

1) Each of the organizations wanted their representative to speak.

    → *Each of the organizations wanted its representative to speak.*

2) Anyone can succeed if they try hard enough.

    → _____

3) Honestly, either of the choices are fine with me.

    → _____

4) Both of them is excited to move to a larger city.

    → _____

5) Sometimes, one of the suspects in a legal case win their freedom.

    → _____

6) No one can determine what will happen to themselves in the future.

    → _____

7) Each children who wants to attend school should have the right to do so.

    → _____

8) Each of the three boys are going to take their dogs to the park to play for a while.

    → _____

    _____

9) Any student who is interested in studying abroad should send in their application.

    → _____

    _____

10) No person can avoid making mistakes; in fact, they will make many mistakes throughout life.

    → _____

    _____

11) It is great to see a student who keeps up with their schoolwork and exercises in their free time.

    → _____

    _____

SKILL 4: IMPROVING CLARITY

A. DEGREES OF COMPARISON

Many TOEFL essay topics ask you to compare or evaluate concepts or things. Let's review how to use adjectives to compare two or more people, places, objects, or ideas.

1. THE COMPARATIVE DEGREE

Use the **comparative degree** + **than** when comparing ONE thing (ex. person, place, object, or idea) to ONE other thing.

- **adjective with one syllable (sometimes two) + er**
  - Ex strong + er = stronger
  - The snake is stronger than the mouse.
  - The earthquake was stronger than the aftershock.
- **more + adjective with three syllables (and often two)**
  - Ex more powerful
  - The snake is *more powerful than* the mouse.
  - The earthquake was *more powerful than* the aftershock.
- **Emphasis:** A way to make both formations more extreme is to add **much** before them.
  - The snake is *much stronger than* the mouse.
  - The earthquake was *much more powerful than* the aftershock.

2. THE SUPERLATIVE DEGREE

Use **the** + **superlative degree** when comparing ONE thing to TWO OR MORE other things.

- **adjective with one syllable (sometimes two) + est**
  - Ex strong + est = strongest
  - The heart muscle may be *the strongest* muscle in the body.
  - The earthquake was *the strongest* one ever recorded here.
- **the most + adjective with two or more syllables**
  - Ex most powerful
  - The heart muscle may be *the most powerful* muscle in the body.
  - The earthquake was *the most powerful* one ever recorded here.
- **Emphasis:** A way to make both formations more extreme is to add **by far** before them.
  - The heart muscle may be *by far the strongest* muscle in the body.
  - The earthquake was *by far the most powerful* one ever recorded here.

> **Note** If a two-syllable adjective ends in "y," change the "y" to an "i" and add "er" to form the comparative. Change the "y" to "i" and add "est" to form the superlative.

Practice 1 — Each statement below compares two groups. Complete the **comparative statements** by using the correct *comparative form* plus *than*.

1) Gorillas are _____*larger than*_____ their cousins, the orangutans. (large)

2) Gorillas have a _____ lifespan _____ orangutans do. (long)

3) Orangutans spend time alone; they are _____ other great apes. (solitary)

4) Orangutans usually have reddish fur; they are _____ other great apes. (colorful)

5) Chimpanzees tend to be _____ other apes. (aggressive)

6) Chimpanzees are _____ bonobos at using tools. (good)

7) Bonobos are much _____ chimpanzees. (peaceful)

8) Within their respective social groups, a female bonobo's social status is _____ a female chimpanzee's social status. (high)

Practice 2 — Each statement below describes one group in comparison to all others. Complete the **superlative statements** by using *the* plus the correct *superlative form*.

1) Gorillas are _____*the largest*_____ of all the primates. (large)

2) Gorillas may also be _____ of all the primates. (shy)

3) Siamang gibbons are _____ of all the apes. (loud)

4) Gibbons can also leap _____ distance–8 meters. (far)

5) Young orangutans depend on their mothers for _____ time of any ape. (long)

6) Scientists disagree about which species of great apes is _____. (smart)

7) Chimpanzees are certainly _____ apes. (violent)

8) Yet chimpanzees and bonobos have _____ facial expressions. (more)

9) Chimpanzees and bonobos may also be _____. (playful)

B. GERUNDS AND INFINITIVES

TOEFL essay questions often ask you to compare or evaluate activities. For example, "Which is better, saving money or spending it?" You can prepare for this type of question by reviewing the use of *gerunds* and *infinitives* in sentences.

1. **FORMING GERUNDS**

    Remember that a *gerund* is a word that looks like a verb but acts like a *noun*. Most gerunds are formed by adding "ing" to the end of the base form of a verb.

VERB	GERUND
drink	drinking
talk	talking
learn	learning

    Some verbs undergo a spelling change when adding the "ing" ending.

    ▶ If the base form of a verb ends with a vowel followed by a consonant, repeat the last letter of the verb before adding "ing."

VERB	GERUND
swim	swimming
stop	stopping
hit	hitting

    ▶ If the base form of the verb ends in the letter "e," drop the "e" before adding the "ing" ending.

VERB	GERUND
love	loving
use	using
state	stating

    Ex *Swimming* is the best way to exercise.
    Loving to talk can be both good and bad.
    Staying awake is hard when one is tired.

2. **FORMING INFINITIVE VERBS**

    To form an *infinitive*, add the word "to" before the base form of a verb. An infinitive verb states an action or condition but does not show tense or person.

VERB	INFINITIVE
know	to know
live	to live
return	to return

3. **USING GERUNDS AND INFINITIVES**

    A gerund can act as a noun, such as a subject or an object. Infinitives usually act as objects.

    Ex *Fishing* is an important industry. (The gerund *fishing* acts as a subject.)
    My brother loves *to fish*. (The infinitive *to fish* acts as an object.)

PRACTICE 1 Fill in each blank space by changing the appropriate verb from the word bank into a *gerund*.

find	fish	solve	grill
read	predict	play	eat
spend	send	save	speak

1) A special childhood memory I have is _____*fishing*_____ with my grandfather and _____*grilling*_____ our catch over a fire.

2) When it comes to money, _____ is wiser than _____.

3) Albert Einstein enjoyed _____ his violin when he had trouble _____ a problem.

4) Good writing skills develop quickly when a person spends time _____ and _____.

5) Surely if scientists can succeed in _____ astronauts to the Moon, they can also succeed in _____ a cure for cancer.

6) The reading passage maintains that _____ fish and meat will become unpopular, but the lecturer counters that _____ such a trend is irrational.

PRACTICE 2 Using your own ideas, add an *infinitive verb* to complete each of the sentences below.

1) It is good ____*to give* food to poor people.____

2) It is wise _____

3) It is unwise _____

4) It is normal _____

5) It is exciting _____

6) It is expensive _____

7) It is necessary _____

C. GERUNDS AND INFINITIVES AS OBJECTS

When an action is the object of a sentence, some verbs can pair with both gerunds and infinitives.

"Like" is one such verb:

I like reading. (gerund) I like to read. (infinitive)

But some cannot:

~~I want reading~~. I want to read.
I enjoy reading. ~~I enjoy to read~~.

1. USING A GERUND AS THE OBJECT OF A SENTENCE

Here are some of the verbs that pair with a gerund when the gerund is used as the object of a sentence. Verbs that pair only with gerunds tend to indicate actual events, and sometimes communication.

enjoy	quit	avoid	consider
appreciate	finish	postpone	discuss
mind	stop	delay	mention
admit	keep	suggest	dislike

Ex The company *keeps growing*.

The family *discussed moving*.

Children in every culture *enjoy playing*.

2. USING AN INFINITIVE AS THE OBJECT OF A SENTENCE

Here are some of the verbs that pair with an infinitive when the infinitive is used as the object of a sentence. Verbs that pair only with infinitives tend to indicate potential events, choices, mental processes, and requests or promises.

hope	promise	attempt	plan
agree	appear	seem	expect
intend	offer	pretend	decide
refuse	fail	want	need

Ex The rescuer *promised to return*.

The scientists *hope to find* an answer.

The dog *remembered to bark* for a treat.

PRACTICE 1 Each of the passages below uses infinitives improperly. Rewrite each passage, pairing the verb with the correct *gerund*.

1) People with ophidiophobia fear snakes. They not only <u>fear</u> *to touch* snakes, but they also <u>dislike</u> *to hear* about snakes. They even <u>avoid</u> *to see* pictures of snakes.

   → *People with ophidiophobia fear snakes. They not only fear **touching** snakes, but they also dislike **hearing** about snakes. They even avoid **seeing** pictures of snakes.*

2) Fears can go away. Some people <u>report</u> *to feel* better when they <u>practice</u> *to face* their fears bit by bit. For example, a person who fears heights can <u>practice</u> *to go* up a small ladder.

   → _____

3) Fears can grow worse over time. Doctors <u>suggest</u> *to confront* what one fears. For example, if one fears open places, he or she should not <u>stop</u> *to go* outside.

   → _____

PRACTICE 2 Use *infinitives* from the box to complete the sentences below.

to go	to answer	to land	to investigate
to see	to end	to talk	to send

1) The space rover attempted _____*to land*_____ on the planet.

2) Scientists hoped _____ the planet and see if it could support life.

3) The public wanted _____ photographs of the planet's surface.

4) The mission promised _____ questions about the planet's atmosphere.

5) Each task appeared _____ as planned.

6) Suddenly, the space rover failed _____ information.

7) After several months, scientists agreed _____ the mission.

8) Soon after, the media forgot _____ about it at all.

D. IMPROVING VOCABULARY

1. CHOOSE THE RIGHT WORDS

When writing, finding the perfect words can be difficult. Many writers tend to use vague or repetitive terms for descriptions. However, if you practice varying your vocabulary by using synonyms, your writing will become more engaging and precise.

Ex
large → huge, immense, giant
depend on → count on, rely on, trust in
important → critical, crucial, essential
disprove → contradict, discredit, refute

2. ELIMINATE UNNECESSARY WORDS

Avoid using vague or unnecessary words to make your writing clearer. Avoid the following words or phrases in your academic writing.

things	really	literally
after all	this means that	the fact that

3. LEARN IDIOMS

An *idiom* is a phrase with a specific meaning that may be unclear if you try to define it word-for-word. In English, reading and writing with clarity and precision require familiarity with idioms such as those in the list below.

A *phrasal verb* is an idiom that consists of either a **verb + preposition** or a **verb + adverb** combination. These phrases often have unique meanings.

Phrasal Verb	Meaning	Idiom	Meaning
break down	*stop working*	account for (something)	*provide an explanation*
come across (something)	*discover*	as long as	*provided that*
cut back on (something)	*consume less*	(to be) better off	*(to be) in a better situation*
do away with (something)	*discard*	in general	*under most circumstances*
find out	*discover*	more or less	*somewhat*
give up	*forfeit*	right away	*immediately*
let (someone) down	*disappoint*	so far	*until now*
point out (something)	*indicate*	take it easy	*relax*

PRACTICE 1 Develop the habit of replacing casual or generic words with more precise words. Below, list possible synonyms underneath each boldfaced word.

materials	disagreeable	belongings	typically	suitable	many
awful	harmful	goods	ordinarily	pleasant	an abundance
type	numerous	excellent	variety	routinely	sort

1) **stuff**
   goods
   _____
   _____

2) **good**
   excellent
   _____
   _____

3) **usually**
   _____
   _____
   _____

4) **a lot**
   _____
   _____
   _____

5) **bad**
   _____
   _____
   _____

6) **kind** (of something)
   _____
   _____
   _____

PRACTICE 2 Use the word bank below to help you fill in the appropriate *idiom* or *phrasal verb*.

| as long as | do away with | give up | broken down |
| so far | find out | cut back on | came across |

1) Shelly decided to _____*do away with*_____ her broken, old computer.

2) Drew's old car has _____ once again due to engine problems.

3) The archaeologist _____ an unusual fossil while digging.

4) You can stay up late, _____ you can wake up on time tomorrow.

5) I must _____ eating candy in order to lose weight.

6) My father encouraged me to never _____ on my dreams.

7) The detectives hope to _____ who committed the crime.

8) Dan has only answered two questions _____, but he will continue working on his test.

E. IMPROVING LANGUAGE

1. SUBJECT-VERB AGREEMENT

When a sentence's main verb agrees with the subject of the same sentence in number and person, the sentence has **subject-verb agreement.** Most of the time, you only have to worry about subject-verb agreement when forming present tense sentences, using helping verbs, and using the irregular verb "be."

> **Ex** *Vultures searches* for dead or dying animals to eat. **X**
> → *Vultures search* for dead or dying animals to eat. **O**
>
> When learning a new language, *listening and speaking is* very important. **X**
> → When learning a new language, *listening and speaking are* very important. **O**
>
> The *collection* of rare books *are* in very good condition. **X**
> → The *collection* of rare books *is* in very good condition. **O**

2. PARALLEL STRUCTURE

Writing with **parallel structure** is using the same grammatical structure for all the actions in a sentence, creating a pattern. Parallel structure is most often used for lists and comparisons.

- *Parallelism and Gerunds*

    There are several ways to list activities, and one of these ways is to use gerunds. If you use gerunds in a list, make sure all elements have the same "ing" ending.

    > **Ex** Bruno enjoys sing*ing*, danc*ing*, and *to* party. **X**
    > → Bruno enjoys sing*ing*, danc*ing*, and party*ing*. **O**
    >
    > I enjoy bik*ing* more than *to* swim. **X**
    > → I enjoy bik*ing* more than swimm*ing*. **O**

- *Parallelism and Infinitive Phrases*

    When listing activities using infinitive phrases, make sure that you are consistent with your use of the "to" that comes before the verb.

    > **Ex** On weekends, I like *to* read, watch movies, and *to* go for walks. **X**
    > → On weekends, I like *to* read, *to* watch movies, and *to* go for walks. **O**
    > → On weekends, I like *to* read, watch movies, and go for walks. **O**
    >
    > **Note** In the sentences above, notice that "to" can be included in each element of the list or it can be included with the first element only. Either way, you must be consistent with your placement of "to" in a list.

Practice 1 Change the verb in parentheses to match the subject of each present tense sentence. Write the correct form of the verb in the space provided.

1) Malcolm ___does___ (do) his homework after school every day.

2) The cat _____ (be) scratching at the door.

3) John and Paul _____ (be) working on a project together.

4) No one _____ (go) to that house because it is haunted.

5) The box of books _____ (collect) dust in the garage.

6) The investigation of the robbery _____ (have) yielded no results.

7) The announcement made by the scientists _____ (state) that the experiment was a success.

Practice 2 Rewrite each sentence on the lines below, fixing any *parallel structure* errors.

1) Jim enjoys playing the guitar and to sing.

   → *Jim enjoys playing the guitar and singing.*

2) In college, I studied literature, physics, and doing math.

   → _____

3) My grandfather enjoys reading, walking, and to sleep.

   → _____

4) A good friend should be honest, be trustworthy, and kind.

   → _____

5) A successful basketball player should be able to pass, dribble, and shooting the ball.

   → _____

6) Ron will receive a promotion because he is very smart, he works hard, and is never late.

   → _____

7) Choosing the right university can be difficult, but to choose the right profession is even harder.

   → _____

F. SOUNDING FORMAL

When listening to conversational English, you might hear people use **contractions** or **reduced forms of verbs**. Avoid using these features of spoken English in formal writing, including in your TOEFL writing section responses.

Ex Baseball is much like life; one ***can't*** do everything oneself.
Even the pitcher ***can't*** do everything by himself or herself. ***It's gotta*** be a team effort. **X**

→ Baseball is much like life; one ***cannot*** do everything oneself.
Even the pitcher ***cannot*** do everything by himself or herself. ***It has got to*** be a team effort. **O**

▶ *Practice*

Replace contractions below with full phrases.

I'm = _____	it's = _____	isn't = _____
I'll = _____	it'll = _____	wasn't = _____
I've = _____	it'd = _____	aren't = _____
I'd = _____	we're = _____	weren't = _____
you're = _____	we'll = _____	don't = _____
you'll = _____	we've = _____	doesn't = _____
you've = _____	we'd = _____	didn't = _____
you'd = _____	they're = _____	can't = _____
he's = _____	they'll = _____	couldn't = _____
he'll = _____	they've = _____	won't = _____
he'd = _____	they'd = _____	wouldn't = _____
she's = _____	there's = _____	haven't = _____
she'll = _____	there're = _____	hasn't = _____
she'd = _____	there'll = _____	hadn't = _____

Another common form in spoken English is the "reduced form" of certain verb phrases. Using reduced forms in your writing makes it informal, so avoid using them in your writing responses.

Ex I'm ***gonna*** go, I'm***unna*** go, or I'm***a*** go. **X**   → I am ***going to*** go. **O**
I've ***gotta*** work or I ***gotta*** work. **X**   → I ***have got to*** work or I ***have to*** work. **O**
I ***wanna*** sleep. **X**   → I ***want to*** sleep. **O**
I'm ***kinda*** busy at the moment. **X**   → I am ***kind of*** busy at the moment. **O**

Practice 1

Rewrite the following sentences, replacing reduced forms and contractions with corresponding *formal phrases*.

1) Eventually, we're gonna use up all the world's fossil fuels.

    → *Eventually, we are going to use up all the world's fossil fuels.*

2) I'm gonna travel for a while after college.

    → _____

3) He didn't wanna run for president again.

    → _____

4) Don't touch the dog when it's eating, or it's gonna bite you.

    → _____

5) The writer probably doesn't wanna point out the drawbacks of the plan.

    → _____

6) It's always gonna be helpful to review topics that you've learned in school.

    → _____

Practice 2

In the following essay, highlight all the *contractions* and underline the *reduced forms*.

> There're special aspects to every time of year, but my favorite season's fall. I've two main reasons for loving fall. One's that after a dry, hot summer, the cool air and rain are a relief, and I just wanna be outdoors. Secondly, during fall, my family starts planning what we're gonna do for the winter holidays. It's always an exciting time, even though we've gotta start a new school year.

Rewrite the paragraph above using correct formal words and phrases.

_____

_____

_____

_____

_____

GRAMMAR SKILLS ♦ CHAPTER 1

G. PHRASES

A **phrase** is a group of words that work together to form a part of speech such as a noun, adjective, or verb. Two of the most common types of phrases are prepositional phrases and participial phrases.

1. PREPOSITIONAL PHRASES

A **preposition** indicates a noun's relationship with another part of the sentence. Usually, prepositions indicate where something is.

Common Prepositions			
up	down	in	at
from	to	with	inside
around	before	upon	along

A **prepositional phrase** begins with a preposition and usually acts as an adjective or adverb.
A comma must be placed at the end of a long prepositional phrase that begins a sentence.

Prepositional Phrases that Act like Adjectives	Prepositional Phrases that Act like Adverbs
The man **in the red jacket** is dating Louise. The house **down the street** is huge.	The car drove **through the tunnel**. **From atop the hill**, Kyle could see the whole city.

2. PARTICIPLES AND PARTICIPIAL PHRASES

Participles: words that look like verbs, but act like adjectives. There are both present participles and past participles.

The **present participle** is formed by adding the "ing" ending to the base form of the verb *(burning, walking, singing)*.

The **past participle** is usually formed by adding the "ed" ending to the base form of a verb *(walked, talked, waited)*. However, some verbs are irregular in their past participle formation.

3. HOW TO USE PARTICIPIAL PHRASES

Participial phrases always begin with a participle, which is followed by modifiers or nouns. A participial phrase will always act as an adjective. There are three ways to place a participial phrase in a sentence:

FORMAT

- **Participial phrase + comma (,) + main clause**
  Gathered by the fire, the campers told stories for hours.
  Hoping to escape the fox, the rabbit dives into a tunnel.

  The participial phrases come right before the nouns that they describe.

- **Main clause + participial phrase**
  Everyone admired the buffalo **grazing peacefully**.
  The manager caught his employee **stealing money**.

  The participial phrases come right after the nouns that they describe.

- **Main clause + comma (,) + participial phrase**
  Jason sat on the bench for hours, **thinking about his life**.
  The bacteria spread rapidly, **thriving in its hot environment**.

  The participial phrases refer to nouns mentioned earlier in the sentence.

Note See the charts below for some of the most common irregular past participles.

verb	past participle	verb	past participle
be	been	go	gone
become	become	have	had
begin	begun	make	made
chose	chosen	prove	proven
come	come	see	seen
do	done	take	taken
feel	felt	tell	told
get	got	write	written

Respond using full sentences and include at least one **prepositional phrase** in each response.

1) Where do you usually do your homework?

   → *I do my homework at my desk.*

2) When do you usually brush your teeth?

   → _____

3) Where do you go to socialize with your friends?

   → _____

4) What time do you wake up in the morning?

   → _____

5) Where might you go to relax by yourself?

   → _____

In each question below, combine the two sentences by making the sentences in bold into a **participial phrase** that corresponds with the second sentence.

1) The ocelot lives deep in South American forests. + The ocelot is a shy nocturnal feline.

   → *Living deep in South American forests, the ocelot is a shy nocturnal feline.*

2) The boys have chosen teams. + The boys begin to play soccer.

   → _____

3) The teacher wrote in red ink. + The teacher made many corrections.

   → _____

SKILL 5: MULTI-PART SENTENCES

A. CLAUSES

Increasing the complexity of your sentences can allow you to express more complicated thoughts and concepts. This section reviews the major components of sentences and explores the ways in which these components relate to one another. A *clause* is a mini-sentence within a sentence; it has a subject and a verb of its own. It can be independent or dependent.

1. INDEPENDENT CLAUSE

An *independent clause* is a clause that could act as a complete sentence.

"I went to the library" is an independent clause because it contains a complete thought with a subject (I) and a verb (went).

2. DEPENDENT CLAUSE

A *dependent clause* is a clause that could not act as a complete sentence. It depends on other information.

"Because I needed to study" is a dependent clause. Although it has a subject (*I*) and a verb (*needed*), it does not form a complete thought by itself.

B. CONJUNCTIONS

Conjunctions connect words, phrases, or clauses to the rest of a sentence.

1. COORDINATING CONJUNCTIONS

Coordinating conjunctions connect thoughts that possess a similar construction. Thus, they show a relationship between two words, phrases, or clauses.

The coordinating conjunctions are *for, and, nor, but, or, yet,* and *so*. They can be remembered using the acronym **FAN BOYS**.

F	for
A	and
N	nor
B	but
O	or
Y	yet
S	so

2. SUBORDINATING CONJUNCTIONS

Subordinating conjunctions introduce dependent clauses and express how a dependent clause relates to the rest of the thought.

Examples of subordinating conjunctions:

if	than	after	since	when
while	until	because	although	where

Practice 1

Combine the two sentences below using *a comma + coordinating conjunction: for, and, nor, but, or, yet, so.* Some may have more than one possible answer.

1) The ancient Egyptians preserved bodies. + They believed that spirits of the dead returned.

   → *The ancient Egyptians preserved bodies, **for** they believed that spirits of the dead returned.*

2) Egyptians covered a body in special salt for weeks. + It would dry out.

   → _____
   _____

3) They added wine, spices, oil, wax, and gum. + Then they wrapped the body in cloth.

   → _____
   _____

4) Before 2000 BCE, Egyptians placed mummies in a wooden box. + Later they began using an inner and outer box.

   → _____
   _____

5) They painted an illustration of the person's face on the box. + The painted faces were often lifelike.

   → _____
   _____

6) They might paint the rest of the box with scenes of gods. + They might paint symbols.

   → _____
   _____

Practice 2

Fill in the blank spots with the appropriate *subordinating conjunctions* from the word bank.

although	when	after
while	because	if

1) Spain controlled Puerto Rico until 1898, ____*when*____ the island became United States territory.

2) _____ nearly 20 years, the U.S. recognized Puerto Ricans as citizens in 1917.

3) _____ the island borders the tropical Caribbean Sea, it also borders the chilly Atlantic Ocean.

4) _____ Puerto Rico mostly used to grow sugar cane, now it has more factories.

5) Puerto Rico is rich _____ one compares it to other Latin American countries.

6) Puerto Rico is also a popular destination for tourists _____ of its warm, tropical weather.

C. COMPOUND AND COMPLEX SENTENCES

1. COMPOUND SENTENCES

Combine independent clauses using *a comma and a coordinating conjunction* or *a semicolon*.

▷ **COMMA with Coordinating Conjunction:**
One way to combine two independent clauses is by using *a comma (,)* followed by *a coordinating conjunction (for, and, nor, but, or, yet, so)*.

> Independent clause + **Comma (,)** + **Conjunction** + Independent clause

Ex The American city of Memphis is called "Home of the Blues," and the city of Nashville goes by "Music City."

▷ **SEMICOLON:**
Another way to combine two independent clauses is by using a **semicolon (;)**.

> Independent clause + **Semicolon (;)** + Independent clause

Ex Nashville's *Grand Ole Opry* is a weekly country music show; it has been on the radio since 1925.

2. COMPLEX SENTENCES

Form *a complex sentence* by combining a dependent clause and an independent clause.

▷ Use a *comma (,)* to separate clauses when a dependent clause comes before an independent clause.

> Dependent clause + **Comma (,)** + Independent clause

Ex Because early settlers in central Tennessee played violins and acoustic guitars, the region became known for its bluegrass and country music sound.

Ex Although Nashville is associated with country music, the city also has deep traditions of gospel, jazz, and blues.

▷ When a dependent clause comes *after* an independent clause, a *comma* between them indicates that the dependent clause provides "extra" information. In other words, if there is a comma, the dependent clause is not essential to the meaning of the sentence.

> Independent clause + **Comma / No Comma (,)** + Dependent clause

Ex Memphis is on the edge of the Mississippi Delta, where African Americans developed the Delta Blues using guitar and harmonica.

Practice 1

Change the sentences below into a *compound sentence* and a *complex sentence* using conjunctions and commas.

1) I am very tired. I still have to study for my test tomorrow.

   Compound: *I am very tired, but I still have to study for my test tomorrow.*

   Complex: *Although I am very tired, I still have to study for my test tomorrow.*

2) Ants are small. Ants are highly efficient workers.

   Compound: _____

   Complex: _____

3) We can go watch a movie. We can go eat dinner.

   Compound: _____

   Complex: _____

4) I will make dinner for myself. I am hungry.

   Compound: _____

   Complex: _____

5) Kelly is always late for school. Kelly received detention.

   Compound: _____

   Complex: _____

6) Janet forgot her wallet at home. Her friend paid for her dinner.

   Compound: _____

   Complex: _____

7) Mark rushed to the supermarket. It closed before he arrived there.

   Compound: _____

   Complex: _____

8) Charles studied for his final exam. He received an "A" on the test.

   Compound: _____

   Complex: _____

D. TRANSITIONS

Beginning a sentence with a *transition word* shows how the information in the sentence relates to previous information.

TRANSITION WORDS

Meaning	Examples
addition	*additionally, furthermore, in addition, in fact, moreover*
cause-and-effect	*as a result, consequently, therefore, to this end*
compare/contrast	*compared to, despite, however, in contrast, on the contrary, on the one hand, on the other hand, nevertheless*
conclusions	*finally, in conclusion, in summary, to conclude, thus, in short*
examples	*for example, for instance, in this case, in this situation*
introductions	*according to, as indicated in/by, based on*
reasons	*one reason is, another reason is, due to*
sequence	*afterward, again, finally, first, next, previously, second, third*

Ex Changes in policy do not disturb Jack. *In fact*, he finds them exciting.

Jason's bicycle is broken. *Therefore*, he will need to borrow Mike's.

Many people love desserts. *For instance*, my whole family loves chocolate cake.

It was a beautiful day. *Nevertheless*, Marissa felt depressed.

Pablo always kept his room very tidy. *In contrast*, his brother's room was always a mess.

Liam's team won the baseball game. *Afterward*, they went to eat pizza together.

Hannah is allergic to pollen. *Consequently*, spring is her least favorite season.

The Amur Leopard is an endangered species of cat. *According to* scientists, only 40 of them remain in the wild.

PRACTICE 1 Use the *transition words* in the word bank to clarify the relationship between the sentence pairs.

> For instance   However   ~~In fact~~   According to

1) Marie Curie was the first woman to be awarded a Nobel Prize. _____In fact_____, she was the only woman to win the prize in two sciences.

2) The Earth's continents have not always looked like they do today. _____ scientists, all the continents were once connected to one another.

3) Not all new businesses become successful. _____, researchers found that 27 percent of new restaurants failed after a year.

4) Penguins move quickly through water because of their body shape, wings, and webbed feet. _____, these same features cause them to move slowly on land.

PRACTICE 2 Use the *transition words* in the word bank to clarify the relationship between the sentence pairs.

> Nevertheless   Thus   Afterward   For example

1) In 1902, President Teddy Roosevelt refused to shoot a captured bear. _____, "Teddy's bears" quickly became popular toys.

2) The wandering albatross has a 3.1-meter wingspan. _____, it can easily glide on wind currents.

3) The Sun is nearly 150-million kilometers away from Earth. _____, the Sun still provides the energy that makes Earth livable.

4) Carlsbad Caverns in New Mexico has incredible cave features. _____, the site contains a rock formation that looks like a waterfall.

TOEFL PATTERN WRITING 1

Chapter 2

PRACTICING INTEGRATED WRITING

GENERAL INFORMATION

A. THE INTEGRATED WRITING TASK

1. EXPLANATION OF TASK

- You will have 3 minutes to read a 250- to 300-word passage that defines an academic term, process, or concept.
- You will use a headset to listen to a 2-minute lecture that either **supports** or **refutes** the information presented in the passage.
- Given a 20-minute response time, you will connect the information in the lecture to the information in the passage.
- Topics on this writing task include academic subjects commonly studied at universities, such as literature, biology, and psychology.

2. NECESSARY SKILLS FOR TASK

To complete the writing task, you must be able to:
- **paraphrase** and **summarize** major points from reading and listening information
- explain the relationships between the major points

3. STRATEGIES FOR APPROACHING TASK

You will receive scratch paper for the writing test, so you can use either paper or the computer's word processor to take notes and form an outline.

1) Take notes as you read the academic passage. After 3 minutes, the passage disappears.
2) Take notes as you listen to the lecture.
3) The writing prompt asks you to summarize and connect information in the passage and the lecture. Then the reading passage reappears.
4) Spend approximately 5 minutes organizing your notes into an outline.
5) Use the remainder of your time to compose a response based on your outline. The suggested response length is 150-225 words. A word counter displays your word count.

4. TIPS

1) Focus on the lecture; determine how the lecture relates to the passage.
2) Do not simply copy text from the lecture and the passage. Copying exact text from either of the sources will result in the deduction of points. Paraphrase the information instead.
3) Respond using simple present tense whenever doing so is appropriate: "The lecture says..."
4) Demonstrate your ability to use transitions, citations, and reporting verbs or phrases.
5) Save the last few minutes of your response time to proofread and edit your essay.

> **Note** The passages and lectures throughout this book are shorter and use simpler language than those you will encounter on the iBT TOEFL.

B. INTEGRATED RESPONSE FORMAT

Ideally, your Integrated Writing response will consist of four paragraphs: an introduction followed by three body paragraphs. There will be two or three main points presented in the lecture that correspond with points from the passage. Each of these will provide the topic for one of your body paragraphs.

Your Integrated Writing response should be formatted something like this.

- **Introduction**
  Topic Statement: presents the passage's and the lecture's main idea and states whether the lecture supports the passage or not

- **Body Paragraph 1**
  provides the first example from the passage and the first example from the lecture that shows support or contrast

- **Body Paragraph 2**
  provides the second example from the passage and the second example from the lecture that shows support or contrast

- **Body Paragraph 3**
  provides the third example from the passage and the third example from the lecture that shows support or contrast

Note Because the passages and lectures in this book are meant to be simpler that those encountered on the TOEFL Writing test, many of the responses in this book have only **three paragraphs**.

C. HACKING STRATEGY – INTEGRATED

1. TAKING NOTES

Take notes on the passage and the lecture, and pay special attention to whether the lecture **supports** or **refutes** the passage.

2. OUTLINING

Organize your thoughts by forming a **topic statement** and identifying three points from the lecture that either support or refute the points from the passage.

3. ESSAY WRITING

Refer to your outline and add **transition words** to clarify the relationship between the passage and the lecture. Summarize, paraphrase, and cite important information.

4. PROOFREADING

Proofread and **edit** your essay by remembering the "Essay Checklist" located on page 74.

GENERAL WRITING SKILLS

A. TAKING NOTES

Note taking is writing down information from sources that you encounter from the reading and listening portions of the Integrated Writing task.

Taking notes involves:
- identifying the **main ideas** and the **important details**

1. ABBREVIATIONS

When taking notes for the Integrated Writing response, save time by using **abbreviations**, which are symbols or shortened forms of words.

Abbreviation/Symbol	Meaning	Abbreviation/Symbol	Meaning
&	and	@	at
%	percent	#	number
ex	example	b/c	because
w/	with	w/o	without
>	more than	<	less than
=	equal, is	→	resulting in
↓	decreasing	↑	increasing
/	or	$	money
+	positive/add	–	through

2. LIST FORMAT

Another way to save time is to **condense information** in your notes. For example, try using a list format to record an outline of the information. Doing so allows you tol leave out transitions, verbs, and other words that you think you will remember anyway.

Passage	Summary Notes
Venus is the second planet from the Sun. The planet's thick atmosphere traps the Sun's heat, so temperatures on the planet's surface can reach over 450 degrees Celsius.	- *2nd planet from Sun* - *thick atm. → 450°C surface*

Read the short passages below. Then fill in the blank lines with notes that contain the most important pieces of information from the corresponding passage.

1)

Passage	Notes
In 1970, there were about 3.5 billion living people. By 2013, the human population had increased to more than 7 billion.	• _____ • _____

2)

Passage	Notes
Explorer Christopher Columbus landed on a Caribbean island in 1492. He had hoped to discover a new trade route to Asia.	• _____ • _____

3)

Passage	Notes
Some Eastern Native American tribes lived in wigwams. They started by cutting young trees and bending them to make dome-shaped frames.	• _____ • _____

4)

Passage	Notes
In December of 1903, the Wright brothers tested their Wright Flyer, which resulted in the first successful airplane flight in history.	• _____ • _____

5)

Passage	Notes
An ecosystem is a set of relationships between living creatures and their surroundings. Thus, an ecosystem can be as small as a pond, or as large as an entire ocean.	• _____ • _____

6)

Passage	Notes
Many ancient societies believed that the gods decided the outcome in games of chance. Thus, many important decisions were made by rolling dice or flipping coins.	• _____ • _____

7)

Passage	Notes
In 1850, California became a state. One reason for this was the discovery of gold in California, which led to a sudden increase in the region's population.	• _____ • _____

8)

Passage	Notes
The setting for a novel may be a *dystopia* – an imagined future in which everyone is miserable. This imagined future often illustrates social issues in the author's own society.	• _____ • _____

9)

Passage	Notes
Learned helplessness is the belief that one cannot solve problems. For example, a student who repeatedly fails tests may feel that studying will not help him do better.	• _____ • _____

10)

Passage	Notes
An autobiography is a story in which an author writes about events from his or her own life. Although the term was created in the 18th century, people have been recording their life stories for many centuries.	• _____ • _____

B. CONNECTING INFORMATION

During the reading and listening portions of the Integrated Writing task, you will read a passage about an academic subject and then listen to a lecture on that subject.

Afterward, you will be asked a question about the connection between the lecture and the passage.

The lecture will either provide information that:

- **supports** the information in the passage
- **refutes** the information in the passage

SUPPORTING

The lecture supports the main idea presented in the passage.

The lecture may:
1. provide examples or explanations that elaborate upon the passage's main idea.
2. provide evidence to prove the passage's main idea.

ARRANGING INFORMATION

The lecture refutes the main idea presented in the passage.

The lecture may:
1. provide examples or explanations that question the passage's main idea
2. provide evidence to disprove the passage's main idea

REFUTING

 Write down whether the lecture topic supports or refutes the passage topic.

1) **Passage Topic**: English scientist Isaac Newton changed how humans understand the universe.
   Lecture Topic: Isaac Newton's ideas established the basis for classical mechanics.

   → *The lecture supports the passage.*

2) **Passage Topic**: Traveling by car is the safest way to travel long distances.
   Lecture Topic: Traveling by airplane is both safer and faster than traveling by car.

   → _____

3) **Passage Topic**: Dog breeds were usually created for a specific purpose.
   Lecture Topic: People bred poodles to obey commands well during a hunt.

   → _____

4) **Passage Topic**: People who smile and move their eyebrows up and down will look friendly.
   Lecture Topic: Gestures are not as important as asking questions that show one's interest in someone.

   → _____

5) **Passage Topic**: The Pacific Ocean's Mariana Trench is the deepest point in Earth's oceans.
   Lecture Topic: The bottom of the trench sits nearly 11 kilometers below the ocean's surface, and water temperatures there are just above freezing.

   → _____

6) **Passage Topic**: Schools have many reasons to teach influential literature, such as *The Great Gatsby*.
   Lecture Topic: Research shows that understanding literature improves a person's level of empathy.

   → _____

C. REPORTING VERBS AND PHRASES

Use **reporting verbs or phrases** to give information from another source. These words indicate that you are reporting what someone else said.

COMMON REPORTING VERBS AND PHRASES

Category	Examples
Indication (neutral)	according to, assert, believe, claim, conclude, describe, discuss, emphasize, explain, express, focus on, indicate, point out, show, state, suggest, write, say
Agreement	agree, confirm, elaborate upon, support
Disagreement	contrast, criticize, disagree, refute, dispute

Ex *According to* researchers, a bloodhound's sense of smell is 1,000 times better than a human's.
The zoologist *confirmed that* monkeys yawn when they see other monkeys yawning.
The research *refuted* the belief that the color red causes bulls to become aggressive.

D. CITING INFORMATION

When you **cite information**, you tell the reader the source of the information you are using. Doing so is not only honest, but it also adds experts' opinions and can strengthen your argument.

METHODS OF CITING INFORMATION

- **Quoting** is using quotation marks (" ") to enclose any phrases or sentences that you copy word-for-word.
- **Paraphrasing** is restating information from the text using different words.
- **Summarizing** is describing basic ideas or main points from the text.

Ex
- **Original Text**: Female lions are usually more skillful hunters than male lions are.
- → **Quote**: *The passage states, "female lions are usually more skillful hunters than male lions are."*
- → **Paraphrase**: *The passage indicates that, among lions, females have better hunting skills than their male counterparts.*
- → **Summary**: *The passage suggests that female lions hunt more effectively than males.*

Read the passage below. Then answer each question.

The Use of Fossils

Fossils are the remains or evidence of ancient organisms. Scientists primarily use fossils to understand extinct plants and animals. They compare the features of ancient fossils to those of living species. For instance, researchers discovered connections between dinosaurs and modern birds by examining dinosaur fossils. They found that some dinosaurs developed bones in their arms that do not look like any bones in modern reptiles. However, these bones are very similar to those found in modern bird wings. Now, it is possible to say that birds are in fact a type of dinosaur.

1) Complete the quote providing a definition for fossils.

   The passage states, "Fossils are _____*the remains or evidence of ancient organisms*_____."

2) Complete the quote stating the main use for fossils.

   According to the passage, fossils are used "to understand _____."

3) Complete the paraphrases of the sentences below by selecting the best synonym for each boldfaced and italicized word.

   a. They *compare* the *features* of *ancient* fossils to those of living species.

      → Scientists (***find similarities between*** / **search carefully for**) the (***characteristics*** / **difficulties**) of (***prehistoric*** / **recent**) fossils and the features of species that are currently alive.

   b. *For instance*, researchers *discovered* connections between dinosaurs and modern birds by *examining* dinosaur fossils.

      → (**For example** / **To conclude**), scientists (**found** / **denied**) links between dinosaurs and living birds by (**studying** / **using**) the features of dinosaur fossils.

   c. They *found* that *some* dinosaurs developed bones in their arms that *do not look like* any bones in modern reptiles. However, these bones are very similar to those found in modern bird wings.

      → Scientists (**determined** / **failed**) that (**certain** / **all**) dinosaurs possessed arm bones that are (**unlike** / **better than**) reptile bones, but similar to bones in the wings of birds.

4) Summarize the main idea of the passage.

   → According to the author, _____

   _____

Read the passage below. Then answer each question.

Benedict Arnold's Viewpoint

Benedict Arnold is considered one of the greatest traitors in American history. However, historians often ignore his motivations for betrayal. Arnold became a top leader in America's Continental Army in 1775, when the American Revolution began. He won important battles with his intelligence and courage. But as the war continued, he often felt betrayed by the Continental Congress, which continually denied him promotions. This caused him to believe that the American leaders were unjust and unqualified. Finally, in 1778 Arnold began giving the British secrets for cash. Soon afterward, his attempt to surrender a Continental fort to the British failed. Arnold then escaped to a British ship.

1) Complete the quote that describes how Benedict Arnold is remembered.

   The passage claims that Arnold "is often considered _____."

2) Complete the quote that describes Arnold's early military career.

   According to the passage, "Arnold became _____," during the onset of the American Revolution.

3) Complete the paraphrases of the sentences below by selecting the best synonym for each boldfaced and italicized word.

   a. He won *important* battles with his intelligence and *courage*. But as the war continued, he often felt betrayed by the Continental Congress, which *continually* denied him promotions.

      → Although Arnold's intellect and (**bravery** / **anger**) won (**significant** / **different**) battles, Continental Congress (**repeatedly** / **finally**) denied him promotions.

   b. He *believed* that the American leaders were *unjust* and *unqualified*.

      → Arnold (**thought** / **wished**) that the leaders of America were (**unfair** / **understandable**) and (**incapable** / **interesting**).

   c. His *attempt* to *surrender* a Continental fort to the British *failed*.

      → Arnold's (**effort** / **regret**) to (**give up** / **take over**) an American military base to British forces (**was unsuccessful** / **was important**).

4) Summarize the main idea of the passage.

   → According to the author, _____

   _____

Read the passage below. Then answer each question.

The Influence of Isaac Newton

In 1687, mathematician and physicist Isaac Newton published his most influential book, the *Principia*. The book laid the foundation for research in mathematics and physics. In three volumes, Newton describes the three laws of motion. For example, he defines the processes that occur when one object strikes another. Newton's *Principia* also contains his law of universal gravitation, which accurately describes how gravity influences the motions of objects. Moreover, the math that Newton used to establish these fundamental laws of physics created the basis for modern calculus.

1) Complete the quote detailing what Newton wrote.

   The author states, "Isaac Newton published _____

   _____," in 1687.

2) Complete the quote that describes the significance of *Principia*.

   The passage claims that the *Principia* "laid the foundation _____

   _____."

3) Complete the paraphrases of the sentences below by selecting the best synonym for each boldfaced and italicized word.

   a. In three volumes, Newton ***describes*** the three laws of motion. For example, he ***defines*** the processes that occur when one object ***strikes*** another.

      → In the *Principia*, Newton (**explains** / **denies**) the three laws of motion. For instance, Newton (**states** / **refutes**) what happens when one thing (**hits** / **limits**) another.

   b. Newton's *Principia* also ***contains*** his law of universal gravitation, which ***accurately*** describes how gravity ***influences*** the motions of objects.

      → Additionally, the *Principia* (**includes** / **controls**) Newton's universal gravitation law that (**correctly** / **falsely**) reveals gravity's (**effect** / **focus**) on an object's movements.

   c. ***Moreover***, the math that Newton used to ***establish*** these fundamental laws of physics created the ***basis*** for modern calculus.

      → (**Furthermore** / **Nevertheless**), the calculations used by Newton to (**create** / **disprove**) his fundamental laws of physics set the (**limitation** / **foundation**) for today's calculus.

4) Summarize the main idea of the passage.

   → According to the author, _____

   _____

SKILL 3: INTEGRATED ESSAY ORGANIZATION

A. THE INTRODUCTION

1. IDENTIFYING RELATIONSHIPS

Remember that your notes for the Integrated Writing task should include:

- the relationship between the lecture and the passage.
- the main ideas, condensed and abbreviated.

2. FORMING A TOPIC STATEMENT

The next step is to plan your essay. The first paragraph of your essay should include a **topic statement** which:

- states the main idea discussed in both the lecture and the passage.
- states whether the lecture supports or refutes the passage.
- may include basic information about why the lecture agrees or disagrees with the passage.

▶ TOPIC STATEMENT BUILDING

PASSAGE

Although private-school tuition can be expensive, giving a child a private-school education has many benefits. Private schools do not have to follow the same highly structured curriculum as public schools, so children at private schools can receive an individualized education.

LECTURE

A public-school education offers many advantages over a private education. Public schools do not charge tuition, allowing families to save money. Furthermore, teachers at public schools often have more educational training, so children may receive a better education.

The passage and the lecture discuss whether public schools or private schools provide a better education. Both the passage and the lecture seem to answer the question, **"Which one provides a better education?"** Once you realize the basic question, you can form a topic statement easily.

Sample Topic Statement: The lecture talks about the benefits of a public school education, which **refutes** the information presented in the passage.

 **PRACTICE 1** For each set of ideas below, complete the topic statement template by including information from the passage and lecture ideas.

1) **Passage Idea**: Some astronomers have believed that the universe is flat in shape.
   Lecture Idea: Recent research indicates that the universe may be shaped like a sphere.

   Topic Statement:

   The lecture discusses _____*the possible shape of the universe*_____.
   This information (**supports** / ***refutes***) information from the reading.

2) **Passage Idea:** Some researchers believe that the Mayan empire declined because the Mayans used up the natural resources around their cities.
   Lecture Idea: Some scholars of Mayan culture believe that constant warfare led to the society's decline, not the overuse of the natural resources.

   Topic Statement:

   The lecture talks about _____.
   Hence, the lecture (**supports** / **refutes**) the reading passage.

3) **Passage Idea**: A few African-American women writers began to publish their works during the second half of the 19th century.
   Lecture Idea: *Incidents in the Life of a Slave Girl*, published in 1861, was the first autobiography written by a woman who had experienced slavery.

   Topic Statement:

   The lecture mainly discusses _____.
   This information (**supports** / **refutes**) the passage.

4) **Passage Idea**: Laws that control *minimum wage* – how high a salary must be – result in fewer available jobs.
   Lecture Idea: Raising the minimum wage does not lead to fewer available jobs because companies just raise prices or cut other costs.

   Topic Statement:

   The lecture talks about _____,
   which (**supports** / **refutes**) information in the reading passage.

B. THE BODY PARAGRAPHS

Each of the Body Paragraphs should:

- introduce one point from the lecture that supports or refutes a corresponding point from the passage.
- explain the relationship between the two points using details from the lecture and the passage.

RESPONSE FORMAT

BODY PARAGRAPH 1 — the first main example or detail from the lecture

For one, the lecture states that _____

This lecture information (**supports** / **refutes**) information from the reading passage because the reading asserts _____

BODY PARAGRAPH 2 — the second main example or detail from the lecture

Additionally, the lecture asserts that _____

These claims (**support** / **refute**) claims made in the passage because the reading passage describes _____

explanation of how the information in the lecture either supports or refutes ideas in the passage

BODY PARAGRAPH 3 — the third main example or detail from the lecture

Finally, the lecture claims that _____

This lecture information (**supports** / **refutes**) information from the reading passage because the passage states _____

Decide whether each Lecture Point supports or refutes each corresponding Passage Point. Next, write a brief body paragraph that summarizes the lecture and passage information and states the relationship between the lecture and the passage.

1) **Passage Point**: Astronomers have concluded that the universe is expanding.

   Lecture Point: In 1929, astronomer Edwin Hubble discovered that galaxies are spreading apart, providing evidence that the universe is indeed expanding.

   The lecture talks about _observations made by Edwin Hubble that prove that galaxies are moving away from each other._ This lecture information (**_supports_** / **refutes**) information from the reading passage because _the passage presents the conclusion that the universe is expanding._

2) **Passage Point**: A professional sports arena brings money into a community.

   Lecture Point: Sports arenas create excessive traffic on game days, leading to more costs than benefits for the community.

   The lecture claims that _____
   _____ This lecture information (**supports** / **refutes**) information from the reading passage because the passage states that _____

3) **Passage Point**: One reason that ancient people feared Vikings was that they fought with iron axes.

   Lecture Point: Vikings were no more violent than other people of the day; Viking axes had many peaceful uses.

   The lecture asserts that _____
   _____ These claims (**support** / **refute**) the passage, which maintains that _____

EXERCISE 1

Read the passage and the **supporting** lecture.

PASSAGE

Toxic Waste Storage

Today's society creates huge amounts of toxic waste. Governments and businesses should avoid storing such poisons underground. Sometimes the poisons are put in underground storage tanks or deep wells. In all cases, the risk of leaks is great. If a toxic substance leaks out, it can get into soil and groundwater. Moreover, if toxic waste is stored underground, people are less able to monitor the waste to make sure that it remains contained. However, if it is stored above ground, people can make ongoing adjustments and repairs to the waste containment facilities.

SUPPORTING LECTURE

When toxic waste is stored underground, leaks are a real possibility. Even the U.S. Environmental Protection Agency has admitted that no current technology can prevent underground leaks forever. And these leaks become nightmares; once rain flows into the ground and spreads the toxin, or once the toxin gets into groundwater, there's no way to clean it up.

Furthermore, it's correct that underground storage is hard to keep an eye on; it's even possible that people could forget where the storage site is. It would be better to explore above-ground waste storage options.

Using the templates below, take notes on the passage and the lecture.

PASSAGE NOTES

Avoid storing toxic waste underground:

- _____
- _____

SUPPORTING LECTURE NOTES

Shouldn't store toxic waste underground:

- _____
- _____

Writing Task

> **Prompt**
> Using the response format below, **summarize** the points made in the **supporting lecture**, being sure to specifically explain how it **supports** the explanations in the passage.

The lecture discusses _____

_____

_____

The lecture supports information presented in the reading passage.

For one, the lecture states that _____

_____

_____

This lecture information supports the information from the reading passage because the passage also describes _____

_____

_____

Additionally, the lecture asserts that _____

_____

_____

These claims elaborate upon the claims made in the passage because the reading mentions _____

_____

_____

EXERCISE 1

Model Answer

M.I. main idea   D1 detail 1   D2 detail 2

PASSAGE

Toxic Waste Storage

M.I. <u>Today's society creates huge amounts of toxic waste</u>. Governments and businesses should avoid storing such poisons underground. Sometimes the poisons are put in underground storage tanks or deep wells. In all cases, the risk of leaks is great. **D1** **If a toxic substance leaks out, it can get into soil and groundwater.** Moreover, **D2** **if toxic waste is stored underground, people are less able to monitor the waste to make sure that it remains contained.** However, if it is stored above ground, people can make ongoing adjustments and repairs to the waste containment facilities.

SUPPORTING LECTURE

M.I. <u>When toxic waste is stored underground, leaks are a real possibility.</u> **D1** **Even the U.S. Environmental Protection Agency has admitted that no current technology can prevent underground leaks forever.** And these leaks become nightmares; once rain flows into the ground and spreads the toxin, or once the toxin gets into groundwater, there's no way to clean it up.

Furthermore, **D2** **it's correct that underground storage is hard to keep an eye on**; it's even possible that people could forget where the storage site is. It would be better to explore above-ground waste storage options.

PASSAGE NOTES

Avoid storing toxic waste underground:

- *poison can leak, get into groundwater*

- *can't monitor; can't repair tanks*

SUPPORTING LECTURE NOTES

Shouldn't store toxic waste underground:

- *no way to stop underground leaks; no way to clean up*

- *can't monitor; could forget loc.*

Model Answer

> **Prompt**
> Using the response format below, **summarize** the points made in the **supporting lecture**, being sure to specifically explain how it **supports** the explanations in the passage.

The lecture discusses the dangers of storing toxic materials underground. The lecture supports information presented in the reading passage.

For one, the lecture states that even professional agencies admit that underground leaks cannot be contained permanently, and any leaked toxins cannot be removed from groundwater. This lecture information supports the information from the reading passage because the passage also describes the dangers of underground toxic leaks.

Additionally, the lecture asserts that it is possible to lose track of an underground storage containers, so the toxic waste cannot be properly supervised. These claims elaborate upon the claims made in the passage because the reading mentions that these underground storage facilities are difficult to monitor and repair if something goes wrong.

EXERCISE 2

Read the passage and the **refuting** lecture.

PASSAGE

Toxic Waste Storage

Today's society creates huge amounts of toxic waste. Governments and businesses should avoid storing such poisons underground. Sometimes the poisons are put in underground storage tanks or deep wells. In all cases, the risk of leaks is great. If a toxic substance leaks out, it can get into soil and groundwater. Moreover, if toxic waste is stored underground, people are less able to monitor the waste to make sure that it remains contained. However, if it is stored above ground, people can make ongoing adjustments and repairs to the waste containment facilities.

REFUTING LECTURE

Underground storage is by far the safest way to contain toxic waste and prevent leaks. There'll always be risks to storing toxic waste, so authorities have to consider which method carries the least risk. Underground storage means that the substances are safe from the impacts of weather.

Moreover, the alternatives to underground storage are more risky. For example, a leak from an above-ground storage container could have a faster, more concentrated effect on nearby people. Burning the poisonous chemicals causes dangerous air pollution. So ultimately, underground waste storage is the best choice.

Using the templates below, take notes on the passage and the lecture.

PASSAGE NOTES

Avoid storing toxic waste underground:

- _____
  _____
  _____

- _____
  _____
  _____

REFUTING LECTURE NOTES

Should store toxic waste underground:

- _____
  _____
  _____

- _____
  _____
  _____

Writing Task

> **Prompt**
> Using the response format below, **summarize** the points made in the **refuting lecture**, being sure to specifically explain how it **challenges** the explanations in the passage.

The lecture discusses _____

_____

_____

The lecture refutes information presented in the reading passage.

    First, the lecture points out that _____

_____

_____

This lecture information contradicts with the information from the reading passage because the passage describes _____

_____

_____

    Additionally, the lecture asserts that _____

_____

_____

These claims refute the passage because the reading emphasizes _____

_____

_____

PRACTICING INTEGRATED WRITING ♦ CHAPTER 2

EXERCISE 2

Model Answer

M.I. main idea   D1 detail 1   D2 detail 2

PASSAGE

Toxic Waste Storage

M.I. <u>Today's society creates huge amounts of toxic waste.</u> Governments and businesses should avoid storing such poisons underground. Sometimes the poisons are put in underground storage tanks or deep wells. In all cases, the risk of leaks is great. **D1** **If a toxic substance leaks out, it can get into soil and groundwater.** Moreover, **D2** **if toxic waste is stored underground, people are less able to monitor the waste to make sure that it remains contained.** However, if it is stored above ground, people can make ongoing adjustments and repairs to the waste containment facilities.

REFUTING LECTURE

M.I. <u>Underground storage is by far the safest way to contain toxic waste and prevent leaks.</u> There'll always be risks to storing toxic waste, so authorities have to consider which method carries the least risk. **D1** **Underground storage means that the substances are safe from the impacts of weather.**

Moreover, the alternatives to underground storage are more risky. **D2** **For example, a leak from an above-ground storage container could have a faster, more concentrated effect on nearby people. Burning the poisonous chemicals causes dangerous air pollution.** So ultimately, underground waste storage is the best choice.

PASSAGE NOTES

Avoid storing toxic waste underground:

- *poison can leak, get into groundwater*

- *can't monitor; can't repair tanks*

REFUTING LECTURE NOTES

Should store toxic waste underground:

- *least risk of leaks;*

  protected from weather

- *no safe alternative:*

  above-ground leaks → ↑ danger;

  burning → air pollution

Model Answer

> **Prompt**
> Using the response format below, **summarize** the points made in the **refuting lecture**, being sure to specifically explain how it **challenges** the explanations in the passage.

The lecture discusses the benefits of storing toxic materials underground. The lecture refutes information presented in the reading passage.

First, the lecture points out that underground storage keeps toxic waste safe from environmental conditions. This lecture information contrasts with the information from the reading passage because the passage describes the dangers of underground toxic leaks, such as the contamination of groundwater.

Additionally, the lecture asserts that storing waste above ground could result in a dangerous, fast-spreading leak, and that the other alternative, burning toxic waste, causes air pollution. These claims refute the passage because the reading emphasizes that leaks in underground storage facilities are difficult to monitor and repair if something goes wrong.

SKILL 4: INTEGRATED ESSAY CHECKLIST

A. PROOFREADING AND EDITING

Here is a checklist to help you review and proofread your integrated essay.

1. ESSENTIALS CHECK

Topic Statement	✓	The topic statement in the introduction summarizes the main idea in the passage and the lecture, and it indicates whether the lecture agrees or disagrees with the passage.
Body Paragraphs	✓	Each paragraph explains how a point from the passage agrees or disagrees with a point from the lecture.
Citations	✓	The source of each borrowed idea is cited. Use citations when you quote, paraphrase, or summarize ideas from another person.
Transitions	✓	Transition words are used effectively between paragraphs and between some sentences to show the relationships between ideas.

2. GRAMMAR CHECK

Subject-Verb Agreement	✓	The correct verb matches the subject of each sentence in terms of number and person.
Pronouns	✓	Each pronoun matches its *antecedent* – the word or words that the pronoun is referring to – in number.
Spelling & Punctuation	✓	The spelling and punctuation are correct.

3. STYLE CHECK

Word/Sentence Variety	✓	Words and the structures of sentences are varied to avoid repetition; synonyms have been used to avoid copying.
Clarity	✓	Ideas and sentences are clearly stated. Word usage is accurate and appropriate.

Using the hint boxes, locate the errors throughout the sample response. Then rewrite the response on the lines below. Check off the errors in the checklist on the side as you correct them in your revised version. Some boxes may remain unchecked.

This sentence has a subject-verb agreement error.

The topic statement does not indicate whether the lecture agrees or disagrees with the passage.

> The lecture **discuss** the benefits of storing toxic materials underground. The passage also talks about underground toxic waste storage.
>
> **However; I think that** underground storage keeps toxic **waist** safe from environmental conditions. This information differs from claims in the reading passage, which state that toxic waste storage can lead to groundwater contamination.

This sentence is missing a citation, uses a transition word incorrectly, and it contains spelling and punctuation errors.

This paragraph does not explain how details from the lecture support information from the passage.

Rewrite

_____
_____
_____
_____
_____
_____
_____
_____
_____
_____
_____
_____
_____

Proofreading Skill	**Check**
Essentials Checklist	
• Topic Statement	
• Body Paragraphs	
• Citations	
• Transitions	
Grammar Checklist	
• Subject-Verb Agreement	
• Pronouns	
• Spelling & Punctuation	
Style Checklist	
• Variety	
• Clarity	

TOEFL PATTERN WRITING 1

Chapter 3

PRACTICING INDEPENDENT WRITING

SKILL 1 — GENERAL INFORMATION

A. THE INDEPENDENT WRITING TASK

1. NECESSARY SKILLS FOR TASK

To complete the writing task, you must be able to:

- form opinions about personal experiences and events.
- organize ideas logically using a clear thesis statement, supporting paragraphs, and a conclusion.
- convey information clearly using correct grammar and appropriate vocabulary.
- use transitions, citations, and reporting verbs or phrases accurately.

2. STRATEGIES FOR APPROACHING TASK

You will receive scratch paper for the writing test, so you can use either paper or the computer's word processor to take notes and form an outline. You have a total of 30 minutes to complete this task.

1) Spend about 5 minutes planning and outlining your essay.
2) Spend about 20 minutes writing your response.
3) Leave a few minutes to proofread and edit your response.

- You must state, explain, and support an opinion about a familiar topic.
- You will receive one of three prompt types:

Type 1 Agree or Disagree Prompts

Do you agree or disagree with the following statement? Use reasons and examples to support your opinion.

Some people believe X. Other people believe Y. Which position do you agree with? Give reasons and details to support your answer.

Type 2 Compare and Contrast Prompts

Some people believe X. Other people believe Y. Compare these two attitudes. Which attitude do you agree with? Give reasons and details to support your answer.

Type 3 Personal Opinion Prompts

Describe a time when X happened in your life. Explain why this event/person/object is so important to you. Use reasons and examples to support your answer.

Note Personal opinion topics will vary in format.

B. INDEPENDENT RESPONSE FORMAT

Because you only have a few minutes to organize your ideas for the Independent Writing response, you should quickly write down ideas using a format that will help you organize your supporting evidence and explanations.

Your essay should consist of either four or five paragraphs: an *introduction*, two to three *body paragraphs*, and a *conclusion*.

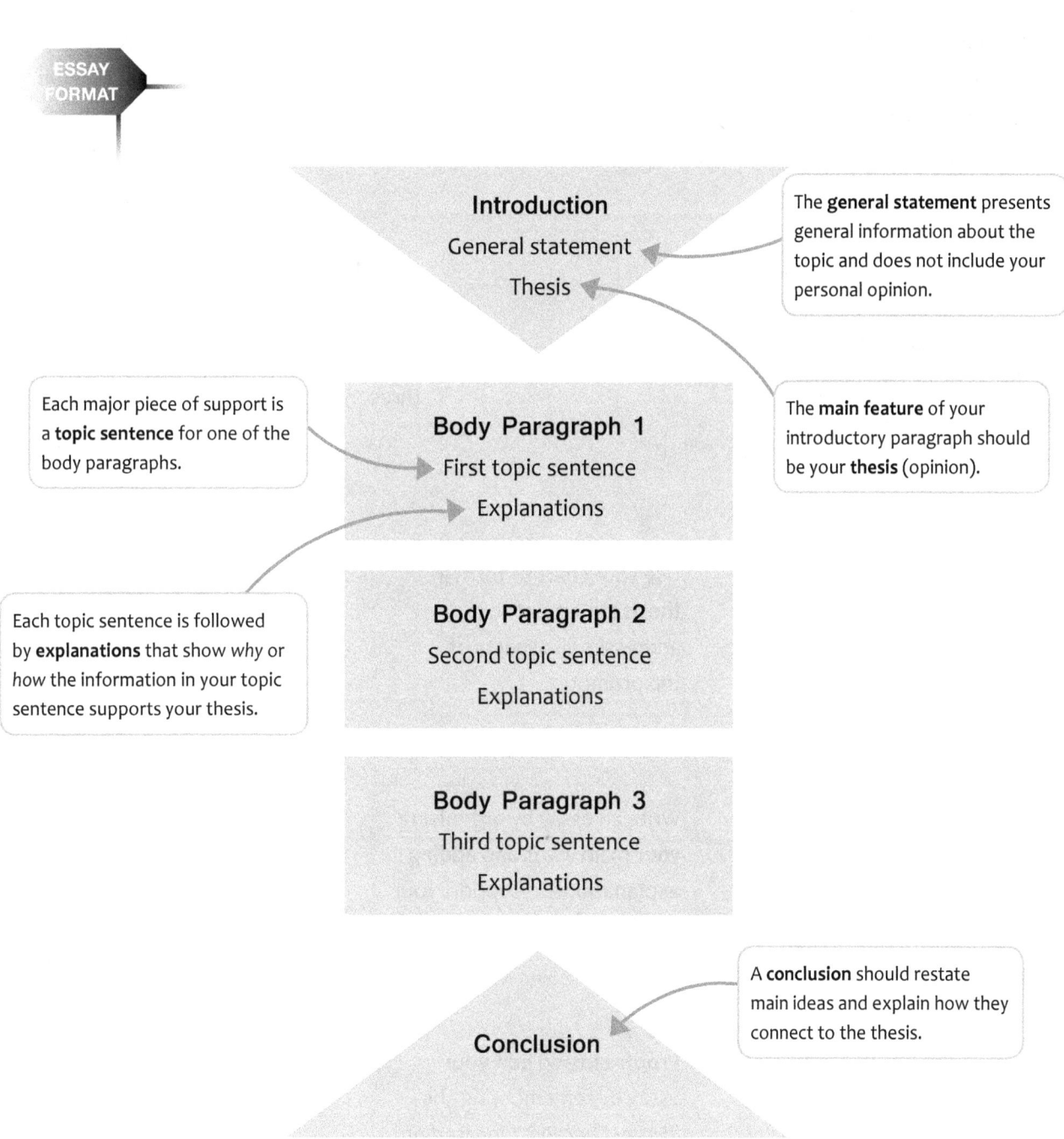

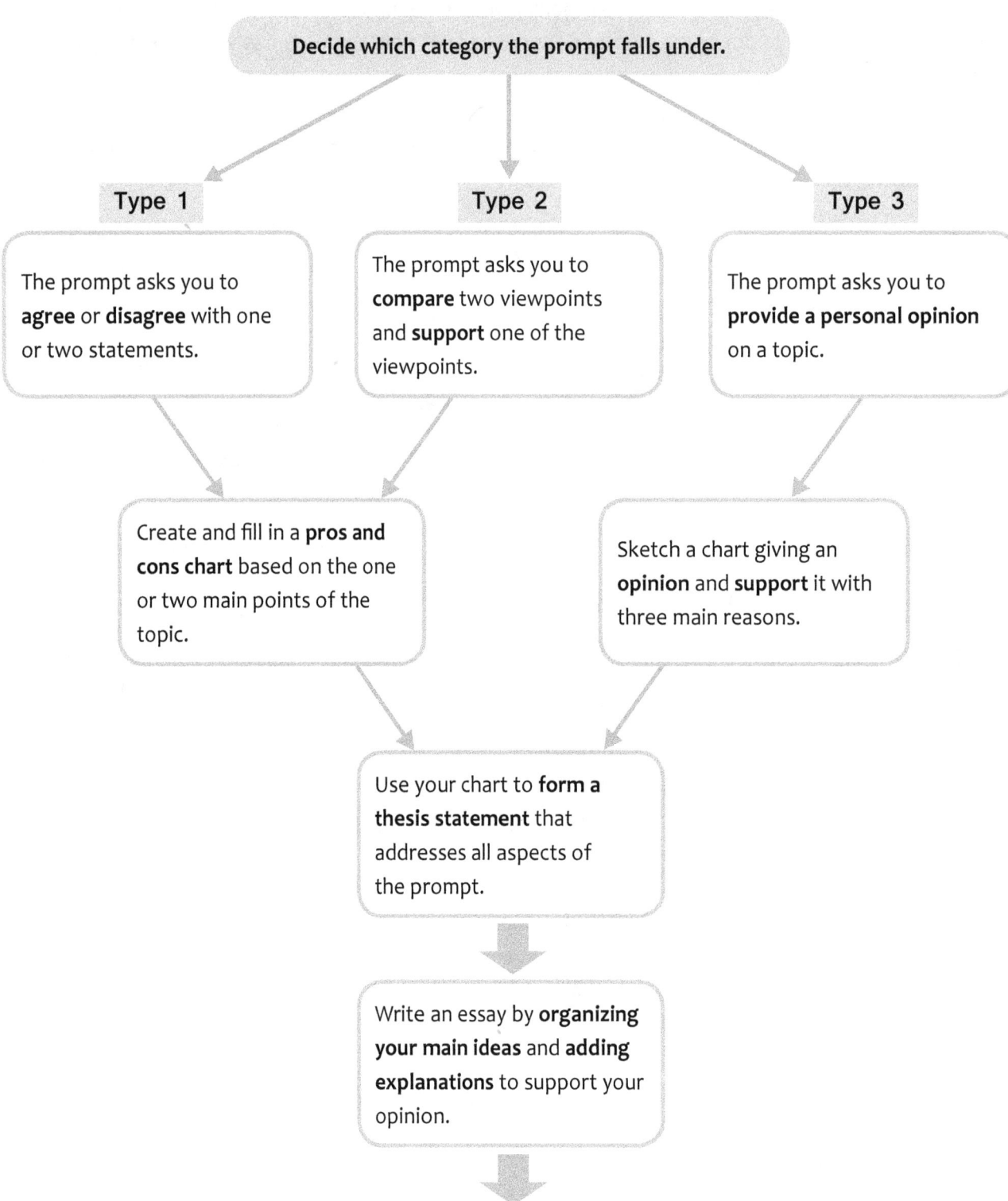

D. INDEPENDENT QUESTION TYPES

TYPE 1: AGREE/DISAGREE PROMPTS

If the Independent Writing prompt asks you to *agree* or *disagree* with a viewpoint, your first task should be to choose a side to defend.

> **EXAMPLE 1**
> Do you agree or disagree with the following statement? Moving to a new house is often better than staying in the same community for a long time. Use examples and details to develop your response.

> **EXAMPLE 2**
> Some people prefer to study one subject intensely for a long time. Other people would rather study many subjects for short periods. Which type of learning do you prefer? Use examples and details to develop your essay.

RESPONSE FORMAT

Introduction
General statement
+
Thesis

Body Paragraph 1
First, **Topic sentence 1**
+
Explanation
+
Explanation

Body Paragraph 2
Second, **Topic sentence 2**
+
Explanation
+
Explanation

Body Paragraph 3
Third, **Topic sentence 3**
+
Explanation
+
Explanation

Conclusion
To conclude,
_____
(Paraphrase **introduction** and expand on main ideas)

TYPE 2: COMPARE AND CONTRAST PROMPTS

Some prompts will ask you to **compare** and **contrast** two viewpoints and then pick a side to support. In these cases, it is often easiest to compare and contrast the two viewpoints in the beginning of your introduction; then you can spend the rest of your response stating why your viewpoint is more valid.

> **EXAMPLE 1**
> Some people prefer to complete school work in study groups. Other people prefer to work by themselves. Compare the advantages of both methods. Which study method do you prefer? Use specific reasons and examples to support your position.

> **EXAMPLE 2**
> Some people prefer to go to bed early in the evening and wake up early in the morning. Other people prefer to stay up late at night and sleep late into the morning. Compare the advantages of each sleep cycle. Which schedule do you prefer? Use specific reasons and examples to support your position.

RESPONSE FORMAT

Introduction
General statement
+
Thesis

Body Paragraph 1
On the one hand, **Topic sentence 1**
+
Explanation
+
Explanation

Body Paragraph 2
On the other hand, **Topic sentence 2**
+
Explanation
+
Explanation

Body Paragraph 3
Moreover, **Topic sentence 3**
+
Explanation
+
Explanation

Conclusion
In conclusion,
_____
(Paraphrase **introduction** and expand on main ideas)

TYPE 3: PERSONAL OPINION PROMPTS

Some prompts will ask for your *personal opinion* about something. The process for outlining these prompts is very similar to the Type 1, agree/disagree prompts discussed earlier.

> **EXAMPLE 1**
> What is your favorite meal or type of food? Use examples and details to develop your essay.

> **EXAMPLE 2**
> What qualities, such as small classes or variety of campus activities, do you look for in a university? Use examples and details to develop your essay.

RESPONSE FORMAT

Introduction
General statement
+
Thesis

Body Paragraph 1
For one, **Topic sentence 1**
+
Explanation
+
Explanation

Body Paragraph 2
Furthermore, **Topic sentence 2**
+
Explanation
+
Explanation

Body Paragraph 3
Finally, **Topic sentence 3**
+
Explanation
+
Explanation

Conclusion
Therefore,
(Paraphrase **introduction** and expand on main ideas)

 # NECESSARY INFORMATION

A. CREATING A PERSONAL PROFILE

You can prepare for the Independent Writing task by studying some of the language that frequently appears in TOEFL writing prompts. To write a successful Independent response, it helps to improve your ability to explain experiences, situations, or thoughts you have had.

Early Experiences

- **Hometown:** *a term that usually refers to the town or city where you grew up; it is a place with which you are familiar and feel "at home"*

  My **hometown** is <u>Hong Kong</u>. I would describe it as (<u>urban</u> / rural / suburban) and (peaceful / <u>exciting</u>).

- **Childhood:** *the time period when a person is a child, especially before the age of 12*

  In my **childhood**, I did not have the technology that today's children have; for example, I did not have <u>a smartphone</u>.

- **To have an influence on:** *to change, affect, or impact someone or something without force*

  A person who **had** a strong **influence on me** when I was growing up was <u>my mother</u>; she taught me that <u>hard work and a commitment to education will lead to happiness and success</u>.

 Read the definition of each vocabulary word. Then answer each question that follows. Circle the choice in parentheses that fits your situation the most closely.

Culture and Society

1) **A trend:** *a direction of change; a current style*

   One positive **trend** in my generation is that people are starting to _____
   _____.

2) **A custom:** *a way that people usually do something in a particular place; a habitual practice*

   A holiday **custom** that I value in my culture is _____ because
   _____.

People and Places

3) **Community:** *refers to an undefined area where people live, or to the people who live there. It may imply an area that is bigger than a neighborhood but smaller than a town.*

   During summer in my **community**, many people enjoy _____
   _____.

4) **A coworker:** *a person with whom you work*

   I would rather have a (**talkative** / **quiet**) **coworker** because _____
   _____.

5) **A roommate:** *someone with whom you share a house, an apartment, or a room*

   I think that the most important quality for a good **roommate** to have is (**cleanliness** / **generosity** / **calmness**) because _____.

6) **A companion:** *someone you spend time with*

   Sometimes, it is (**more fun** / **less fun**) to visit a new place with **a companion** because _____
   _____.

Analysis and Opinion

7) **Beneficial/harmful:** *describing something good or bad*

   It (**is** / **would be**) (**beneficial** / **harmful**) for me to have a job right now because _____
   _____.

8) **Qualities:** *parts or features of a person, place, or thing, especially positive ones*

   (**Honesty** / **Loyalty**) is a more important **quality** in a friend than (**honesty** / **loyalty**) because
   _____.

9) **Characteristics:** *features that are typical of something or someone; distinguishing traits*

   The most important **characteristic** of an excellent teacher is the ability to (**challenge** / **inspire**) students because _____
   _____.

10) **Perspective** or **viewpoint:** *an individual's way of thinking about something*

    My **perspective** on jobs and careers comes from my past experiences, including _____
    _____.

B. CREATING A TIMELINE

Independent Writing prompts often ask you to discuss personal experiences. Developing a timeline of your life can help refresh your memories. It is also a way to practice using English to talk about periods in your life.

Ex Write your profile in the blank space provided using your own words.

TIMELINE

- I was born in Pusan, South Korea.

- When I was 2 years old, my little brother was born.

- At the age of 5, I began learning English with a tutor.

- In kindergarten, I met my best friend, Joon; I felt less shy after that.

- Sadly, when I was 10 years old, my grandfather died; he had a positive influence on me, and I miss him.

- I started playing on my middle school's soccer team.

- I broke my ankle and experienced many challenges moving around.

- During winter break when I was 15, my family and I visited the Philippines.

- While I was in my first year of high school, my older sister left to go to college in Beijing.

- After high school graduation, I started attending college in Seoul.

- At 20, I am applying for business administration programs at various colleges and universities in the United States.

PRACTICE 1 Complete a timeline of your own life. You can add as many events as you like.

TIMELINE

- I was born in _____
- _____
- _____
- _____
- _____
- _____
- _____
- _____
- _____
- _____

INTRODUCTION

A. INTRODUCTION FORMAT

The introduction of an essay is formed by combining a *general statement* and the *thesis*.

The *general statement* introduces the prompt that you will discuss throughout your response. It should be the first one or two sentences of your introduction, and it **should present information broadly.**

The *thesis* is your response to a writing prompt. A thesis should be a single sentence located in the introduction that states an opinion that fully responds to the essay prompt **without including minor details.**

B. BRAINSTORMING IDEAS

When brainstorming and writing an Independent response, you must **choose one viewpoint** that you can develop using details and explanations.

When brainstorming your response, address the three steps that follow:

1) Decide on *an opinion* that answers the question in the prompt. If the prompt asks for your personal opinion, make sure that you choose one opinion that you can then build upon. If the prompt asks you to pick a preference or to agree/disagree with a statement, make sure that you choose a position that you can write about in-depth.

2) Choose two or three ideas that support your viewpoint; you will use these ideas to form *topic sentences* for your body paragraphs, which prove why your thesis is valid.

3) Support your ideas with *explanations*, which provide specific information that relate your support to your thesis.

Your *brainstorm chart* should list simplified versions of your viewpoint, topic sentences, and explanations. Thus, you can remember what you want to include in your final response.

 **PRACTICE 1** Fill in the Notes and Brainstorm charts provided below by adding your own explanations and examples.

> **Prompt**
> Reading is the best way to pass the time.

Notes

agree	disagree
thought-provoking activity	~~exercise is healthier~~
helps you succeed academically	~~time w/ friends = more social~~

Brainstorm

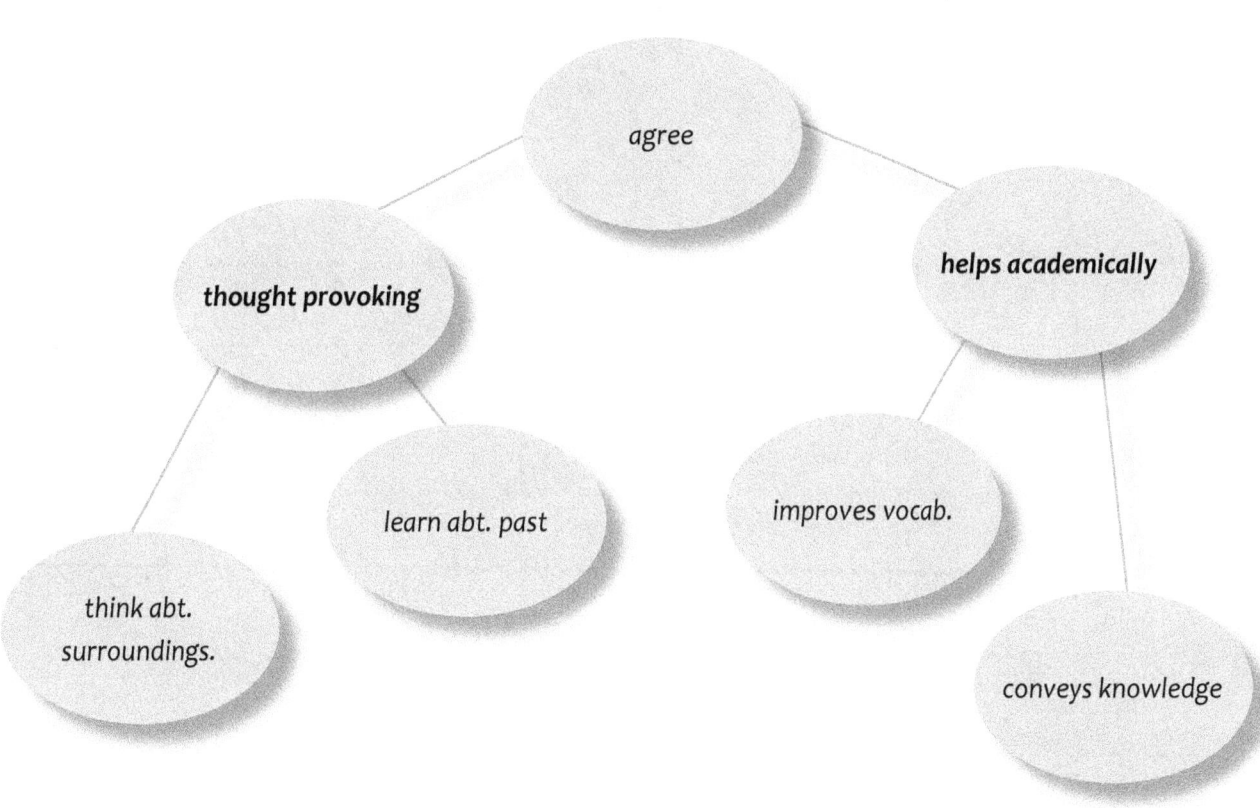

- agree
  - thought provoking
    - think abt. surroundings.
    - learn abt. past
  - helps academically
    - improves vocab.
    - conveys knowledge

PRACTICE 2 Fill in the Notes and Brainstorm charts provided below by adding your own explanations and examples.

> **Prompt**
> Summer is the best season of the year.

Notes

agree	disagree
_____	_____
_____	_____

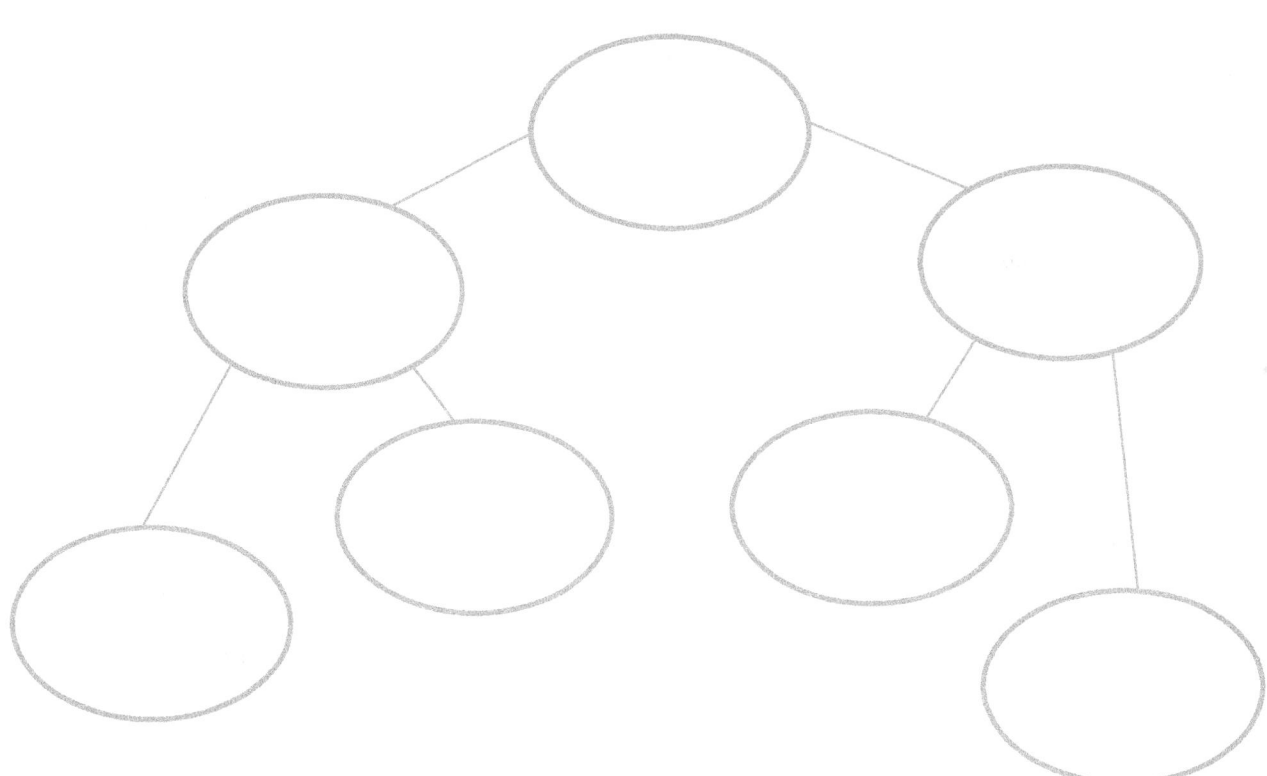

PRACTICE 3 Fill in the Notes and Brainstorm charts provided below by adding your own explanations and examples.

> **Prompt**
> Some people prefer to live in a hot climate while others prefer to live in a cold climate. Compare the advantages of these two living situations. Which do you prefer?

Notes

hot climate better	cold climate better
_____	_____
_____	_____

Brainstorm

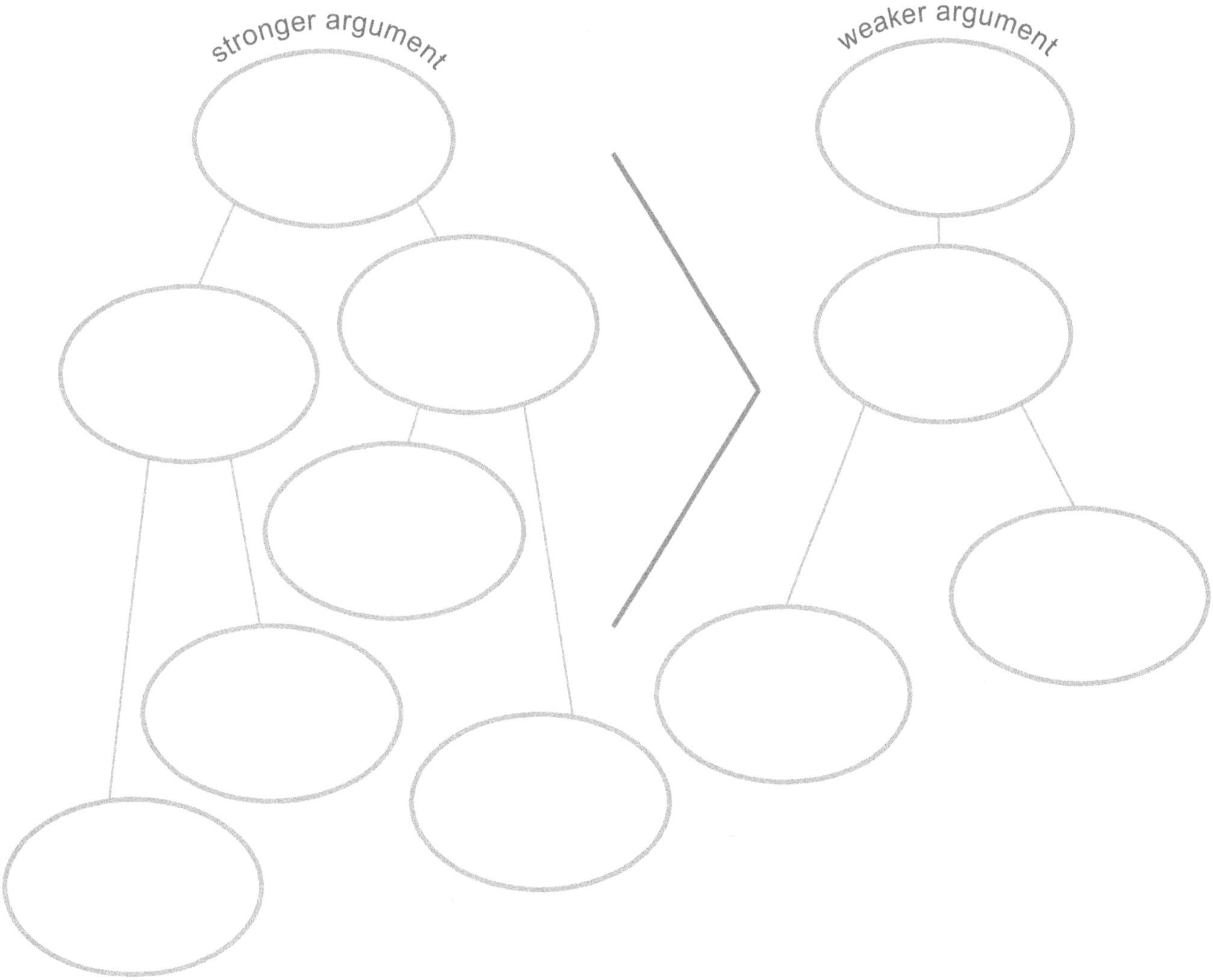

stronger argument

weaker argument

PRACTICE 4 Fill in the Notes and Brainstorm charts provided below by adding your own explanations and examples.

> **Prompt**
> What is the most important subject to study in school?

Notes

Thesis: The most important academic subject is _____.

Reasons:

- _____
- _____

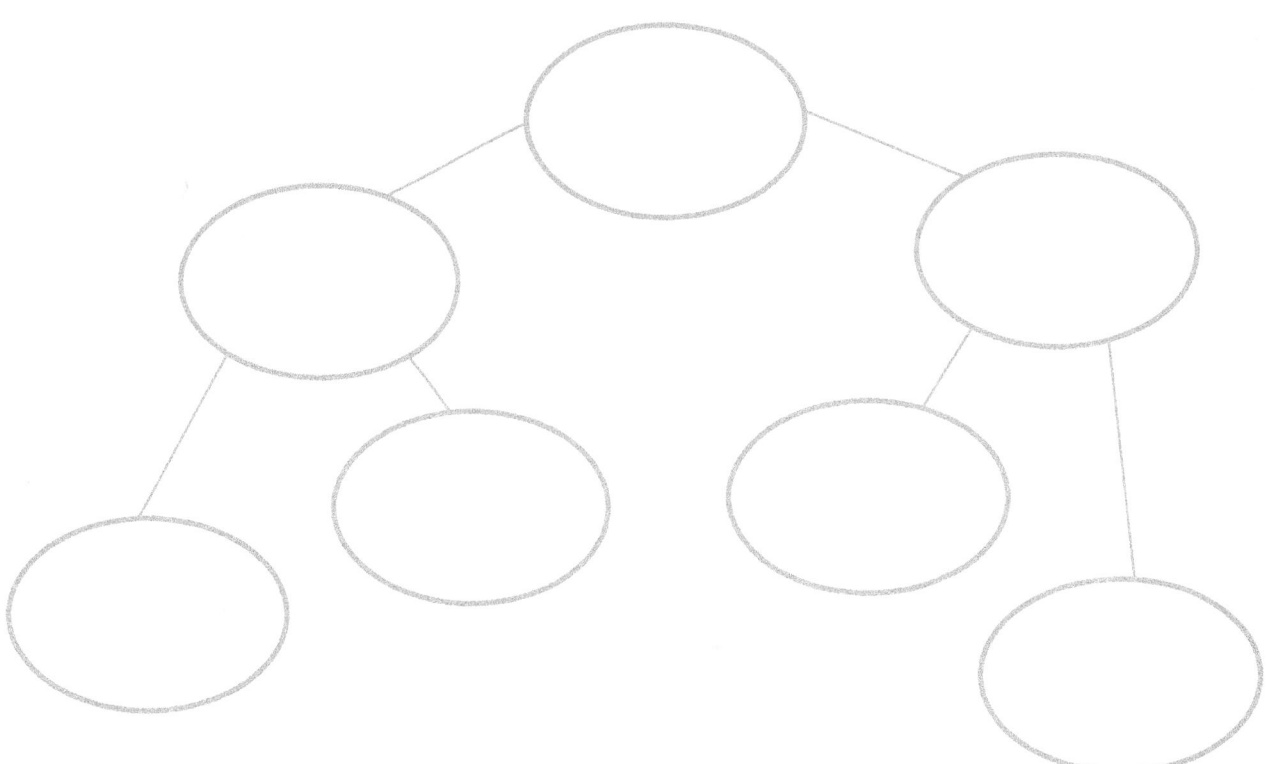

PRACTICE 5 Fill in the Notes and Brainstorm charts provided below by adding your own explanations and examples.

> *Prompt*
> Spending time with friends is more important than studying.

Notes

agree	disagree
_____	_____
_____	_____

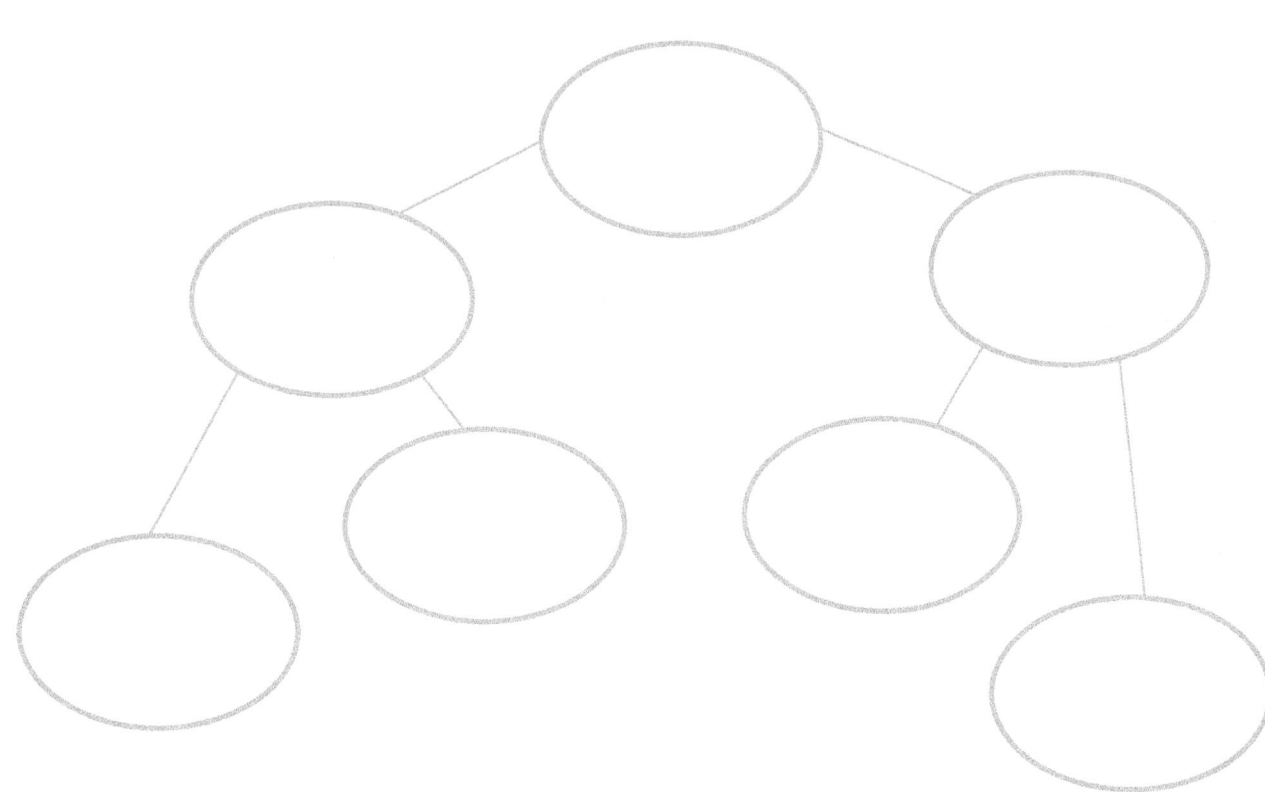

PRACTICE INDEPENDENT WRITING ♦ CHAPTER 3

C. GENERAL STATEMENTS

A *general statement* consists of one or two sentences that set up your essay. As the name implies, it should contain general information that introduces the reader to the topic.

There are an infinite number of ways to form a general statement, but two of the most common are:

1. Ask the reader a broad, thought-provoking question or series of questions that relate to the prompt.

   > **Prompt**
   > Do you agree or disagree with the following statement? Reading is the best way to pass the time.

   Viewpoint: I agree that reading is the best way to pass the time.

   > **Introduction = General Statement + Thesis**
   >
   > **GENERAL STATEMENT** Is the best way to pass the time by doing something fun, or by doing something educational? Finding a good leisure activity can be a major challenge. **+ THESIS** Ultimately, reading is the best way to pass the time because this activity promotes academic success and introduces thought-provoking issues.

2. Acknowledge the side of the argument that disagrees with your viewpoint. Then you can immediately state the side of the argument that agrees with your viewpoint and defend your viewpoint throughout the rest of your response.

   > **Prompt**
   > Do you agree or disagree with the following statement? Reading is the best way to pass the time.

   Viewpoint: I agree that reading is the best way to pass the time.

   > **Introduction = General Statement + Thesis**
   >
   > **GENERAL STATEMENT** Today's society offers many rewarding ways to pass time. Many people enjoy playing video games with friends or watching television programs. **+ THESIS** However, I believe that reading is the best way to pass the time because this activity promotes academic success and introduces thought-provoking issues.

D. THE THESIS

The **thesis** introduces the main argument that you will support throughout your essay. Thus, a thesis must contain an idea that you can justify with explanations for an entire essay.

1) First, take the main idea from the prompt and rephrase it to serve as the introduction to your thesis statement. Thus, the first part of you thesis should simply state your opinion.

> **Prompt**
> Do you agree or disagree with the following statement? Reading is the best way to pass the time.

Thesis beginning: *Reading is the best way to pass the time…*

2) You can use your **Notes** to help form the second part of your thesis, which briefly explains why you selected your opinion.

agree	disagree
thought-provoking activity	~~exercise is healthier~~
helps you succeed academically	~~time w/ friends = more social~~

Select key phrases from each of your main points; these key phrases will be the reasons that support your opinion.

Summary of "agree": *…because this activity promotes academic success and introduces thought-provoking issues.*

3) Now you have all the pieces you need to form a thesis:

- The first part of your thesis should address the prompt.

    Reading is the best way to pass the time…

- The second part of your thesis should give general reasons to support your statement. Use the summary of "agree" from Step 2.

    …because this activity promotes academic success and introduces thought-provoking issues.

4) Put the two parts of the sentence together and you get a well-developed thesis:

   Reading is the best way to pass the time because this activity promotes academic success and introduces thought-provoking issues.

PRACTICE 1

Agree or Disagree

Completely fill in both sides of the chart. Then use these ideas to create an introduction that consists of *a general statement* and *a thesis*.

1) **Prompt**
Do you agree or disagree with the following statement? Every child should have to play a sport.

agree	disagree
build a good work ethic	~~distract from schoolwork~~
keep students out of the street	~~take away from family time~~

Introduction

GENERAL STATEMENT Some people claim that sports distract children from more important responsibilities, such as completing their homework or spending time with their family. **+**
THESIS Personally, I believe that every child (**should** / should not) have to play a sport because sports prevent children from getting in trouble by teaching them about the benefits of hard work.

2) **Prompt**
Do you agree or disagree with the following statement? Having siblings is better than being an only child.

agree	disagree
_____	_____
_____	_____

Introduction

GENERAL STATEMENT _____
_____
_____

+ THESIS I believe that having siblings (**is** / **is not**) better than being an only child because
_____

3) **Prompt**

Do you agree or disagree with the following statement? The best place to make new friends is at school.

agree	disagree
_____	_____
_____	_____

Introduction

GENERAL STATEMENT _____

_____

_____

+ **THESIS** In my opinion, the best place to make new friends (**is** / **is not**) at school because

_____

4) **Prompt**

Do you agree or disagree with the following statement? Doing well in school requires more effort than maintaining a career.

agree	disagree
_____	_____
_____	_____

Introduction

GENERAL STATEMENT _____

_____

_____

+ **THESIS** I think that doing well in school (**does** / **does not**) require more effort than maintaining a career because _____

_____

Compare and Contrast

Completely fill in both sides of the chart. Then use these ideas to create an introduction that consists of *a general statement* and *a thesis*.

1) **Prompt**
Some people prefer to live in a large city while others prefer to live in the countryside. Compare the advantages of each living situation. Which do you prefer?

pros of living in a city	pros of living in the countryside
more entertainment	~~relaxing lifestyle~~
more job opportunities	~~can enjoy nature~~

Introduction

GENERAL STATEMENT Many people enjoy living far away from the hectic lifestyle of a big city, as they have more opportunities to relax and enjoy nature. Yet others prefer a more fast-paced lifestyle. ✚ **THESIS** I believe that living in a large city (**is** / is not) better than living in the countryside because <u>a large city is filled with entertainment and many job opportunities.</u>

2) **Prompt**
Some people prefer to begin working right after high school while others prefer to attend a university. Compare the advantages of each. Which decision do you prefer?

pros of working right after high school	pros of attending college
_____	_____
_____	_____

Introduction

GENERAL STATEMENT _____
_____
_____

✚ **THESIS** In my opinion, getting a job right after high school (**is** / **is not**) preferable to attending a university because _____
_____

3) **Prompt**
Some people prefer to travel alone while others prefer to travel with their friends and family. Compare the advantages of both approaches. Which do you prefer?

pros of traveling alone	pros of traveling with others

Introduction

GENERAL STATEMENT _____
_____
_____

+ **THESIS** Personally, I prefer to travel (**alone / with others**) because _____
_____

4) **Prompt**
Some students prefer to work while they attend a university, yet others prefer to focus all their attention on studying. Compare the advantages of each. Which do you prefer?

pros of working while in school	pros of not working while in school

Introduction

GENERAL STATEMENT _____
_____
_____

+ **THESIS** Personally, I believe that (**working / not working**) while attending school is preferable because _____
_____

Practice 3

Personal Opinion

Completely fill in both sides of the chart. Then use these ideas to create an introduction, consisting of *a general statement* and *a thesis*.

1) **Prompt**
What quality is most important to you in a friend?

Opinion: The quality I value the most in a friend is _____honesty_____.

Reasons:
- *able to trust friend with secrets*
- *should tell me when I'm wrong*

Introduction

GENERAL STATEMENT Is a great friend someone who is polite, or is it someone who takes risks by being honest and ethical? **+ THESIS** The quality I value the most in a friend is *honesty*, because *an honest friend will keep my secrets and tell me when I am wrong*.

2) **Prompt**
Where is your favorite location to visit on vacation?

Opinion: My favorite place to visit on vacation is _____.

Reasons:
- _____
- _____

Introduction

GENERAL STATEMENT _____
_____
_____

+ THESIS My favorite place to visit on vacation is _____
because _____
_____

3) **Prompt**
What are some of the major motivations for a person to attend a university?

Motivations:

- _____
- _____

Introduction

GENERAL STATEMENT _____
_____
_____

+ **THESIS** I believe that a person might want to study at a university because _____
_____

4) **Prompt**
Where is the best place to spend time with friends?

Opinion: The best place to spend time with friends is _____.

Reasons:

- _____
- _____

Introduction

GENERAL STATEMENT _____
_____
_____

+ **THESIS** In my opinion, the best place to socialize is _____, because
_____
_____

# SKILL 4

THE BODY PARAGRAPHS AND CONCLUSION

A. INCLUDING EXPLANATIONS

To complete a body paragraph, you must provide **explanations** that demonstrate how your topic sentences support your thesis.

> **Prompt**
> Do you agree or disagree with the following statement? Reading is the best way to pass the time.

Reasons for Topic Sentences

agree	disagree
thought-provoking activity	~~exercise → healthier~~
helps you succeed academically	~~time with friends → more social~~

The **thesis** is the main idea of the entire essay, so it should be placed in the introduction. Each of the "agree" statements in the chart above can be used as the **topic sentences** to the essay's body paragraphs.

Thesis: Reading is the best way to pass the time because this activity promotes academic success and introduces thought-provoking issues.

To have enough information to complete your body paragraphs, you must provide **explanations** to prove that your topic sentences are valid points.

Explanations are details, examples, or supporting pieces of information. They can be personal experiences that help prove a point, or they can be literary or scientific pieces of information that provide evidence for an opinion.

Topic Sentence 1: Reading is a thought-provoking activity.

Explanation(s):

1. Reading requires a person to visualize information from the text.
2. Readers gain glimpses into the lives of real people and fictional characters.

 Write down TWO *explanations* that support the topic sentence.

1) **Topic Sentence**: Enjoying your job is important to achieving success.

   Explanation 1: *You are likely to devote more time to an activity that you enjoy doing.*

   Explanation 2: *You will put in more effort at a job that you find interesting and enjoyable.*

2) **Topic Sentence**: The Internet has greatly improved people's lives.

   Explanation 1: _____

   Explanation 2: _____

3) **Topic Sentence**: The library is the best place to study.

   Explanation 1: _____

   Explanation 2: _____

4) **Topic Sentence**: Reading a newspaper is the best way to catch up on current events.

   Explanation 1: _____

   Explanation 2: _____

5) **Topic Sentence**: Swimming is the best way to exercise.

   Explanation 1: _____

   Explanation 2: _____

6) **Topic Sentence**: Breakfast is the best meal of the day.

   Explanation 1: _____

   _____

   Explanation 2: _____

   _____

7) **Topic Sentence**: Watching television is not a waste of time.

   Explanation 1: _____

   _____

   Explanation 2: _____

   _____

8) **Topic Sentence**: Receiving good grades improves a student's self-esteem.

   Explanation 1: _____

   _____

   Explanation 2: _____

   _____

9) **Topic Sentence**: Compassion is the best quality for a leader to have.

   Explanation 1: _____

   _____

   Explanation 2: _____

   _____

10) **Topic Sentence**: Universities should allow students to create their own majors.

    Explanation 1: _____

    _____

    Explanation 2: _____

    _____

Read the prompt, thesis, and topic sentences that have been provided. Then add **explanations** to complete the body paragraphs.

> **Prompt**
> Do you agree or disagree with the following statement? Public speaking is a practical life skill to develop. Support your response with relevant details and examples.

Thesis: *I believe that public speaking is a helpful skill, as it improves confidence in the workplace and in one's social life, and it helps develop other important skills.*

Topic Sentence 1: For one, developing public speaking skills improves a person's ability to perform well in situations related to professional life.

Explanation 1: *Being able to convey ideas clearly allows one to represent the company well and is likely to impress supervisors.*

Explanation 2: _____

_____

_____

Topic Sentence 2: Additionally, good public speaking skills can be incredibly useful in social situations.

Explanation 1: _____

_____

_____

Explanation 2: _____

_____

_____

Topic Sentence 3: Finally, developing public speaking skills will naturally improve other important skills.

Explanation 1: _____

_____

_____

Explanation 2: _____

_____

_____

B. THE CONCLUSION

The last major piece of an Independent Writing response is the conclusion. The **conclusion** is the last paragraph of your essay. In the conclusion, you should summarize the main points presented in your body paragraphs and clarify how each of these main points relates to your thesis.

- Do *not* introduce new main ideas or examples in your conclusion.

PARAPHRASE → RESTATE → EXPAND

You can create a conclusion by restating your thesis and main ideas using **paraphrasing** and **summary**. Then you can conclude your essay by offering further details or examples that demonstrate how your thesis relates to everyday life.

> *Prompt*
> Do you agree or disagree with the following statement? Reading is the best way to pass the time.

Thesis: *Reading is the best way to pass the time because this activity promotes academic success and introduces thought-provoking issues.*

Formula for a Conclusion	Example
1) **Paraphrase** your thesis to remind the reader what your essay focuses on.	*Because it increases intelligence and can be done virtually anywhere, reading is the best way to pass time.*
2) **Restate** the main ideas that you used to support your thesis throughout the essay.	*Reading challenges one to imagine different ways of living and experiencing the world.*
3) **Expand** on your main ideas by telling the reader how your support relates to real-life experience.	*Therefore, reading makes it easier to "step into others' shoes" and identify with their life experiences.*

Conclusion: *Because it increases intelligence and can be done almost anywhere, reading is the best way to pass time. Reading challenges one to imagine different ways of living and experiencing the world. Therefore, reading makes it easier to "step into others' shoes" and identify with their life experiences.*

PRACTICE 1 Write a *conclusion* that corresponds to each prompt and thesis provided below.

1) **Prompt**
When choosing a place to live, what do you consider most important?

Thesis: A good living situation is worth searching for, so proper location, adequate size, and an affordable price are the features I consider.

To conclude, *finding a home that is in a good spot, is big enough, and is affordable greatly affects my happiness. If all of these factors fall into place, I know I have found a "perfect fit."*

2) **Prompt**
People try to reduce their stress in many different ways. For example, some may exercise while others may meditate. In your opinion, what is the best way to reduce stress? Use specific reasons and examples to support your answer.

Thesis: I think that exercising is the best way to relax because exercise helps me relieve stress and maintain good health.

In conclusion, _____
_____
_____

3) **Prompt**
Do you agree or disagree with the following statement? Children should learn a foreign language once they start school. Use specific reasons and examples to support your answer.

Thesis: I believe that children should start learning a foreign language as they start school because doing so will allow them to experience different cultures and improve their communication abilities.

Overall, _____
_____
_____

EXERCISE

Read the writing prompts provided below. Then use the template provided below to outline all the information you need to create an Independent Writing response.

> *Prompt*
> Where is one place that you have always wanted to visit? Use specific reasons and details to explain your answer.

Use this space to create a **thesis statement** and to write down your ideas for **topic sentences**.

Notes

Thesis: I want to visit _____.

1) _____

2) _____

Now use your notes from above to create a brainstorm that includes **explanations**, such as details or examples, that show how your topic sentences support your thesis.

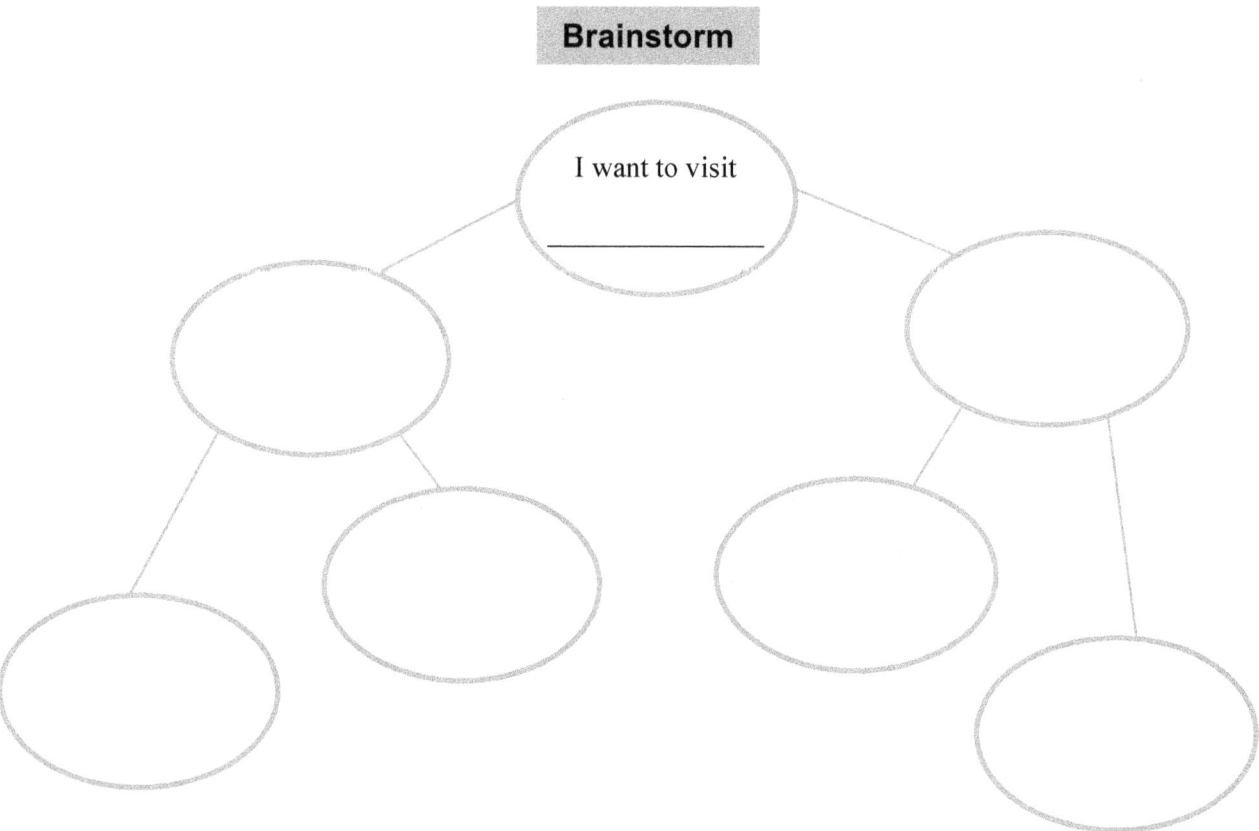

Writing Task

Using your Brainstorm outline from the previous page for guidance, create a full Independent Writing response that includes transition words and explanations.

_____

_____

_____

One place I have always wanted to visit is _____

because _____

_____

    One reason I want to visit _____ is that

_____

_____

_____

    Additionally, I want to visit _____ because

_____

_____

_____

    Therefore, _____

_____

_____

EXERCISE

Model Answer

▸ **Prompt** ◂
Where is one place that you have always wanted to visit? Use specific reasons and details to explain your answer.

Notes

Thesis: I want to visit ___New York City___

1) ___see the Statue of Liberty___
2) ___view the exhibits at famous institutions___

Brainstorm

- I want to visit *New York City*
  - Statue of Liberty
    - 1 of the most recog. symbols of U.S.
    - see it in person
  - exhibits @ famous inst.
    - Metro. Museum of Art & Amer. Museum of Nat. Hist.
    - impressive hist. buildings

Model Answer

The world is filled with places that are fascinating culturally and historically, so choosing just one to visit is no easy task. One place I have always wanted to visit is New York City because the huge city holds so many interesting cultural icons and attractions for tourists to explore.

One reason I want to visit New York City is that I would like to see the Statue of Liberty, which stands on an island in the middle of New York Harbor. It is one of the most recognizable symbols of the United States. The statue also symbolizes the possibility of freedom and justice, so it is meaningful for many of the world's citizens.

Additionally, I want to visit New York City because I would like to view some of the collections on display at the city's world-famous museums, such as the Metropolitan Museum of Art and the American Museum of Natural History. Furthermore, the city is home to impressive historical buildings that guests can tour, such as the Empire State Building and the Guggenheim Museum.

Therefore, New York City is one of the places I have always hoped to visit. It is a city full of unique sites, such as the Statue of Liberty, and it is home to so many museums and monuments that I would love to see in person.

SKILL 5: INDEPENDENT ESSAY CHECKLIST

A. PROOFREADING AND EDITING

Here is a checklist to help you review your independent essay.

1. ESSENTIALS CHECK

Introduction	✓	The general statement mentions the main topic discussed in the essay, and the thesis in the introduction addresses the prompt and presents a viewpoint.
Topic Sentence	✓	Each body paragraph has a topic sentence that supports the thesis statement and provides a main idea for the paragraph.
Explanations	✓	Each body paragraph contains explanations such as examples, details, or reasons that support the main idea of the paragraph.
Transitions	✓	Transition words are used between paragraphs and between sentences to show the relationship between ideas.
Conclusion	✓	The conclusion summarizes the main points and connects them to the thesis.

2. GRAMMAR CHECK

Subject-Verb Agreement	✓	The correct verb matches the subject of each sentence.
Pronouns	✓	Each pronoun matches its *antecedent* – the word or words that the pronoun is referring to – in number.
Spelling & Punctuation	✓	The spelling and punctuation are correct.

3. STYLE CHECK

Word/Sentence Variety	✓	Words and the structures of sentences are varied to avoid repetition.
Clarity	✓	Ideas and sentences are clearly stated. Word usage is accurate and appropriate.

Practice 1

Using the hint boxes, locate the errors throughout the passage. Then rewrite the passage on the lines below. Check off the errors in the checklist on the side as you correct them in your revised version.

New York City is a huge city with interesting neighborhoods and cultural attractions.

Finally, I want to visit New York City because the Statue of Liberty is what I want to see? He is one of the most recognizable symbulls of the United States. Although I have seen many photography of the enormous statue, I would like to sees it in person

Therefore, there are many fascinating cities I would enjoy visiting, some of which include Paris, London, and Los Angeles.

— The thesis does not address the topic.

— This paragraph has an inaccurate transition word, a clarity issue, a punctuation error, a misused pronoun, a spelling error, and a subject-verb agreement error.

— The conclusion does not relate to the introduction or the body paragraph.

Rewrite

_____

_____
_____
_____
_____
_____
_____
_____
_____
_____
_____
_____
_____

Proofreading Skill	Check
Essentials Checklist	
• Introduction	
• Body Paragraphs	
• Conclusion	
• Transitions	
Grammar Checklist	
• Subject-Verb Agreement	
• Pronouns	
• Spelling & Punctuation	
Style Checklist	
• Variety	
• Clarity	

PRACTICE INDEPENDENT WRITING ♦ CHAPTER 3

TOEFL PATTERN WRITING 1

Chapter 4

ACTUAL PRACTICE

TOEFL iBT Integrated Writing Task Rubric

5	• The response effectively identifies relevant information from the lecture and connects it to the related information in the reading in a logical and skillful manner. • The response is well organized and has few grammatical errors. • Any minor errors do not make the content unclear, including the explanation of the reading and lecture relationships.
4	• Meaningful information from the lecture and the reading is presented, and connections between the two are generally accurate, but there may be some minor inexact, incorrect, or omitted information. • A response at this level may have more frequent or apparent minor language errors, but the usage and grammar rarely affect the precision, coherency, or connection between ideas.
3	The response contains important lecture information and relays some critical information between the lecture and the reading. However, the response also contains one or more of the following issues: • The connections between the lecture and the reading are vague, unclear, or generalized. • The response may fail to mention one main point from the lecture. • Some main points from the lecture or reading may be incomplete, incorrect, or imprecise. • Grammatical errors may be more frequent. • Grammatical errors may create unclear connections and result in imprecise expressions.
2	The response provides some important lecture information but reflects major language problems. The response may misstate or omit ideas from the lecture or the connections between the lecture and the reading. One or more of the following may occur: • The response inaccurately represents or leaves out the unifying connection between the lecture and the reading. • The response leaves out or misstates main ideas from the lecture. • Language errors or misused expressions make connections or meaning unclear at critical points in the response.
1	One or more of the following may occur: • The response offers no or little important or relevant information from the lecture. • The intended meaning of the response is unclear.
0	• The response simply copies sentences from the reading. • The response is not related to the topic. • The response is written in a language other than English or only consists of keystrokes.

TOEFL iBT Independent Writing Task Rubric

5	For the most part, the essay accomplishes all of the following points: • The response completely addresses the topic and handles the task effectively. • The response is effectively developed and is well organized. • Examples, explanations, and/or details are appropriate and clearly stated. • The response demonstrates coherence, integration, and appropriate organization. • The entire response shows skill in language usage. This includes the ability to vary sentence structures and use the correct idioms. Minor grammatical or vocabulary errors may occur.
4	For the most part, the essay accomplishes all of the following points: • The response addresses the topic and handles the task well. Some points may not be completely addressed. • In general, the response is well organized and well developed. • Explanations, examples, and/or details are appropriate and clearly stated. • The response demonstrates coherence, integration, and appropriate organization. Occasional repetitions or imprecise connections may occur. • The response shows skill in language usage. The response varies sentence structure and vocabulary usage. Occasional minor errors may occur but do not impact meaning. Errors may include those relating to composition, word form, or idiomatic language usage.
3	The essay is identified by one or more of the following: • The essay responds to the topic and handles the task. Explanations, examples, and/or details are somewhat developed. • The response demonstrates coherence, integration, and appropriate organization. Connections between concepts may be vague at times. • Unclear meanings may result from incorrect sentence formation and word choice. • The response may show a limited, although accurate, range of vocabulary and sentence structures.
2	The essay has one or more of the following issues: • The response is limited in development. • The organization is poor, and/or the connections between concepts are weak. • The response has incorrect or too few examples, explanations, or details to support generalizations. • The choice of words or word forms is obviously incorrect. • Sentence structures and/or word usage errors are common.
1	The essay has serious issues, including one or more of the following: • The response is seriously disorganized or not developed enough. • The response does not demonstrate relevant use of details, or it shows a misunderstanding of the prompt. • There are many major errors in the sentence structure or usage.
0	• The essay does not relate to the topic. • The essay is written in a language other than English, is unwritten, or consists of keystrokes.

Integrated Writing Task

PASSAGE

Welfare Programs

In the United States, government programs that provide financial assistance are called *welfare programs*. Although these programs are supposed to improve society, they are largely ineffective. First, welfare programs do not benefit working Americans even though their taxes pay for these programs. Furthermore, many individuals on welfare do not work because of alcohol or drug abuse; these individuals should not receive government funding to pay for their addictions.

LECTURE

Contrary to what critics claim, welfare programs don't simply hand out money to every unemployed adult. One of the primary goals of many welfare programs is to provide some income to homes with children or elderly people who otherwise couldn't support themselves. Additionally, all welfare programs make sure that capable adults seek job training before receiving financial aid, which encourages them to join the workforce.

PASSAGE NOTES

Welfare programs are (**effective** / **ineffective**) because:

- _____
  _____
  _____

- _____
  _____
  _____

LECTURE NOTES

Welfare is (**helpful** / **not helpful**) to society because:

- _____
  _____
  _____

- _____
  _____
  _____

RESPONSE

20:00 min

> **Prompt**
> Summarize the points made in the lecture, being sure to explain how they relate to specific points made in the passage.

The lecture discusses _____

_____

In doing so, the lecture **(supports / refutes)** information presented in the passage.

For one, the lecture states that _____

_____

_____

This point **(supports / refutes)** claims in the passage, which state that _____

_____

_____

_____

Additionally, the lecture asserts that _____

_____

_____

These claims **(support / refute)** claims made in the passage because the passage

asserts that _____

_____

_____

ACTUAL PRACTICE ♦ CHAPTER 4

Integrated Writing Task

M.I. main idea   **D1** detail 1   **D2** detail 2

PASSAGE

Welfare Programs

M.I. In the United States, government programs that provide financial assistance are called *welfare programs*. Although these programs are supposed to improve society, they are largely ineffective. First, **D1** welfare programs do not benefit working Americans even though their taxes pay for these programs. Furthermore, **D2** many individuals on welfare do not work because of alcohol or drug abuse; these individuals should not receive government funding to pay for their addictions.

LECTURE

M.I. Contrary to what critics claim, welfare programs don't simply hand out money to every unemployed adult. **D1** One of the primary goals of many welfare programs is to provide food and housing to families with children so that the children can build happy, healthy futures and contribute to society. Additionally, **D2** all welfare programs make sure that capable adults seek job training before receiving financial aid, which encourages them to join the workforce.

PASSAGE NOTES

Welfare programs are (**effective** / ***ineffective***) because:

- *workers' taxes pay for welfare but they don't benefit*
  _____
  _____

- *sometimes give $ to addicts*
  _____
  _____

LECTURE NOTES

Welfare is (***helpful*** / **not helpful**) to society because:

- *supports children for future*
  _____
  _____

- *promotes job training for unemployed*
  _____
  _____

MODEL ANSWER

The lecture discusses the benefits of welfare programs. In doing so, the lecture refutes information presented in the passage.

For one, the lecture states that welfare programs help those who cannot support themselves, such as children. This point refutes claims in the passage, which state that welfare programs do not benefit the taxpayers who fund them. However, the lecture points out that children will pay taxes in the future, as well as contribute to society in many other ways.

Additionally, the lecture asserts that adults start preparing for jobs before they receive welfare assistance, which forces some welfare recipients to decrease drug dependency. These claims refute claims made in the passage because the passage asserts that welfare programs give money to people who are unemployed drug addicts.

SYNONYM PRACTICE

Using the word bank below, find two synonyms to match each word in the list below. Then write the corresponding synonyms on the lines provided.

1)	supply	take	give	receive
2)	acceptance	aid	help	agreement
3)	useless	important	valuable	unsuccessful
4)	help	train	support	teach
5)	main	major	famous	popular

1) provide   *supply*   *give*

2) assistance

3) ineffective

4) benefit

5) primary

Independent Writing Task

> **Prompt**
> Do you agree or disagree with the following statement? By using educational technology, students today can learn more information in less time than they could in the past. Use specific reasons and examples to support your answers.

agree	disagree
_____	_____
_____	_____

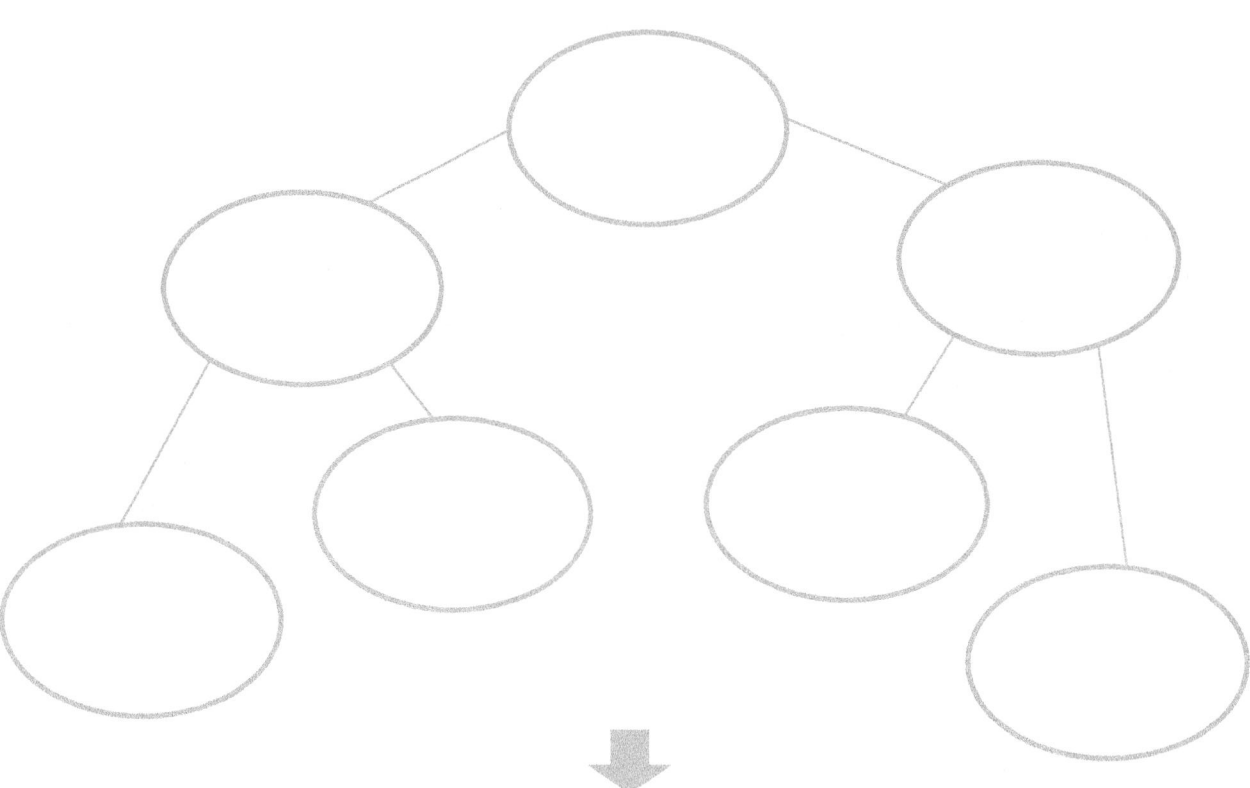

> **Thesis**
> Today's students (**can** / **cannot**) learn more information in less time with the help of technology because _____
> _____.

RESPONSE 30:00 min

_____

_____

Today's students (**can** / **cannot**) learn more information in less time with the help of technology because _____

_____

    First, technology (**helps** / **does not help**) students learn because _____

_____

_____

_____

_____

    Second, technology (**helps** / **does not help**) students learn because _____

_____

_____

_____

_____

    Therefore, _____

_____

_____

Independent Writing Task

> **Prompt**
> Do you agree or disagree with the following statement? By using educational technology, students today can learn more information in less time than they could in the past. Use specific reasons and examples to support your answers.

agree	disagree
provides far-reaching access to info.	*info. less trustworthy (Internet)*
appealing presentation of info.	*more distracting presentation*

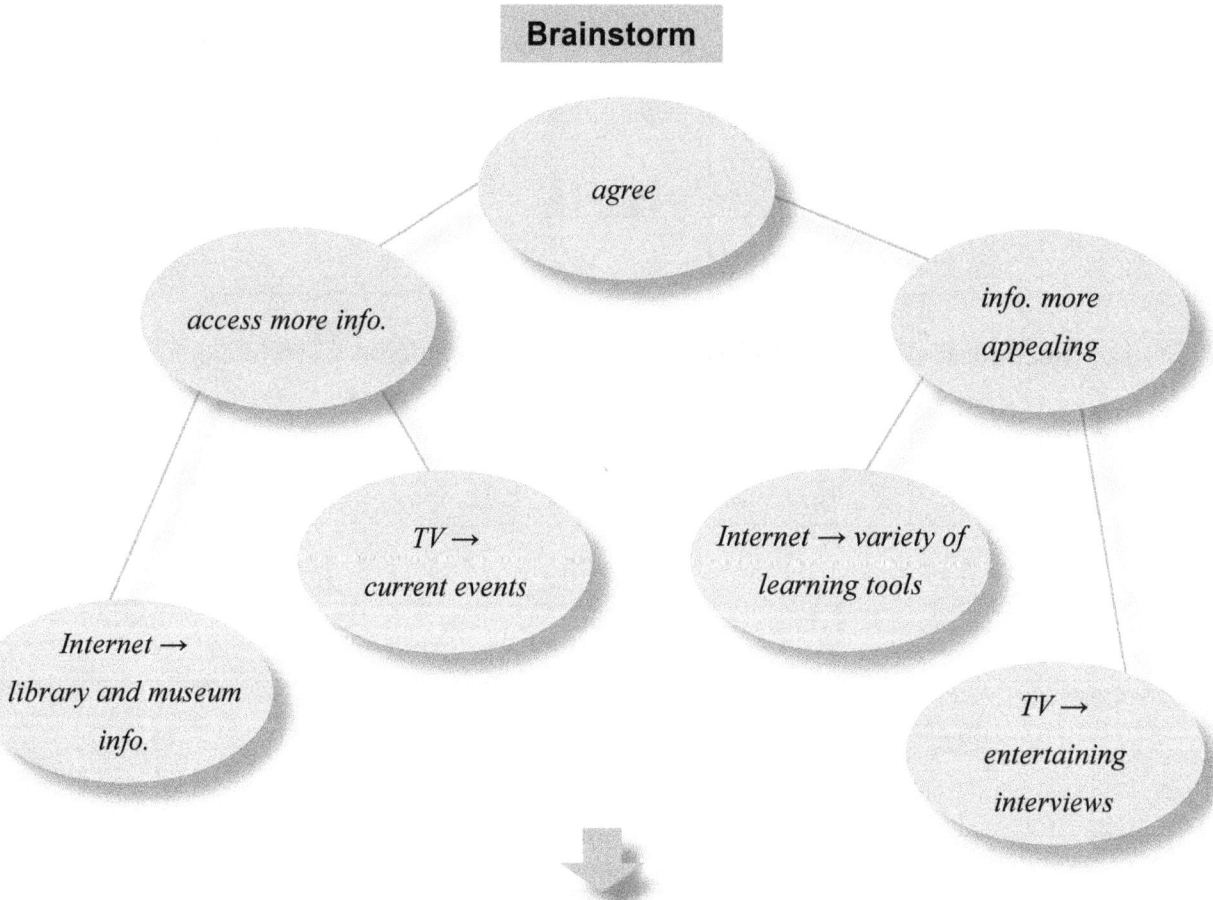

> **Thesis**
> Today's students (*can* / **cannot**) learn more information in less time with the help of technology because *they can access huge amounts of information presented in interesting ways.*

MODEL ANSWER

Technology has improved the way students approach learning. Today's students can learn more information in less time with the help of technology because they can access huge amounts of information that are presented in interesting ways.

First, technology helps students learn because it gives students access to levels of information that were unheard of in the past. For example, the Internet provides instant access to information in libraries and museums from around the world. Even 25 years ago, students were limited to filmed or printed material that a library happened to have on its shelves. Likewise, mass media such as television gives students access to more current events than ever before. Students can watch programs offering different views from countries around the world.

Second, technology helps students learn because modern technology delivers information in a variety of appealing ways. For example, many websites have video clips, audio clips, and pictures related to the same subject. Information is also presented using games, which motivate students to learn. Likewise, television offers documentaries and interviews with experts to make learning interesting. Ultimately, students are able to learn information easily.

Therefore, technology helps students access information and learn it quickly. Resources from the Internet and television even deliver information in a variety of engaging ways so that it is more memorable.

Integrated Writing Task

PASSAGE

Dinosaur Extinction

For decades, scientists wondered why the dinosaurs went extinct about 65 million years ago. In the 1980s, two scientists discovered geological evidence of a meteor impact that occurred at the same time as the dinosaurs' mass extinction. A decade later, researchers identified a massive impact crater in Mexico that supported the idea that a meteor impact caused environmental changes that killed off the dinosaurs.

LECTURE

Although there's some evidence that a meteor impact killed the dinosaurs, this is neither the only nor the best theory of dinosaur extinction. For example, the "geological evidence" mentioned in the passage may have also resulted from a massive volcanic eruption. This eruption would've caused changes to the environment that would've also killed off the dinosaurs and many other species.

PASSAGE NOTES

The major event that occurred 65 million years ago: _____

Evidence for meteor impact causing extinction:

- _____
- _____

LECTURE NOTES

The lecture (**accepts** / **questions**) the meteor extinction theory.

Other theories about dinosaur extinction include:

- _____
- _____

RESPONSE

20:00 min

> *Prompt*
> Summarize the points made in the lecture, being sure to explain how they relate to specific points made in the passage.

The lecture discusses _____

_____

The lecture **(supports / refutes)** information presented in the reading passage.

For one, the lecture states that _____

_____

_____

This lecture information **(supports / refutes)** information from the passage because

the passage implies that _____

_____

_____

Additionally, the lecture asserts that _____

_____

_____

These claims **(support / refute)** claims made in the passage because the reading

suggests that _____

_____

_____

ACTUAL PRACTICE ♦ CHAPTER 4

Integrated Writing Task

M.I. main idea **D1** detail 1 **D2** detail 2

PASSAGE

Dinosaur Extinction

M.I. For decades, scientists wondered why the dinosaurs went extinct about 65 million years ago. In the 1980s, **D1** two scientists discovered geological evidence of a meteor impact that occurred at the same time as the dinosaurs' mass extinction. A decade later, **D2** researchers identified a massive impact crater in Mexico that supported the idea that a meteor impact caused environmental changes that killed off the dinosaurs.

LECTURE

M.I. Although there's some evidence that a meteor impact killed the dinosaurs, this is neither the only nor the best theory of dinosaur extinction. For example, **D1** the "geological evidence" mentioned in the passage may have also resulted from a massive volcanic eruption. **D2** This eruption would've caused changes to the environment that would've also killed off the dinosaurs and many other species.

PASSAGE NOTES

The major event that occurred 65 million years ago: _extinction of dinosaurs_

Evidence for meteor impact causing extinction:

- _geo. evidence from 1980s_

- _crater from meteor found in Mexico, 1990s_

LECTURE NOTES

The lecture (**accepts** / *questions*) the meteor extinction theory.

Other theories about dinosaur extinction include:

- _volcanic eruption → same conditions as meteor impact_

- _env. damage to dinos_

MODEL ANSWER

The lecture discusses a possible cause for the extinction of the dinosaurs about 65-million years ago. The lecture refutes information presented in the reading passage.

For one, the lecture states that there are multiple possibilities for the cause of the geological evidence linked to dinosaur extinction. This lecture information refutes information from the passage because the passage implies that geological discoveries prove that a giant meteor colliding with Earth caused the dinosaurs' extinction.

Additionally, the lecture asserts that a volcanic eruption could have caused the changes to the environment that could have killed all the dinosaurs. These claims refute claims made in the passage because the reading suggests that the meteor theory was proven when researchers discovered what could be an impact crater dating to the time of dinosaur extinction.

SYNONYM PRACTICE

Using the word bank below, find two synonyms to match each word in the list below. Then write the corresponding synonyms on the lines provided.

1)	studied	found	uncovered	reviewed
2)	action	proof	clue	movement
3)	huge	quick	large	rapid
4)	belief	idea	fact	truth
5)	make	create	discuss	state

1) discovered _____ _____

2) evidence _____ _____

3) massive _____ _____

4) theory _____ _____

5) mention _____ _____

Independent Writing Task

> **Prompt**
> A large company will donate money to either support the arts or protect the environment. Which option do you think that the business should support? Use specific reasons and examples to support your answer.

donate to the arts	donate to the environment
_____	_____
_____	_____

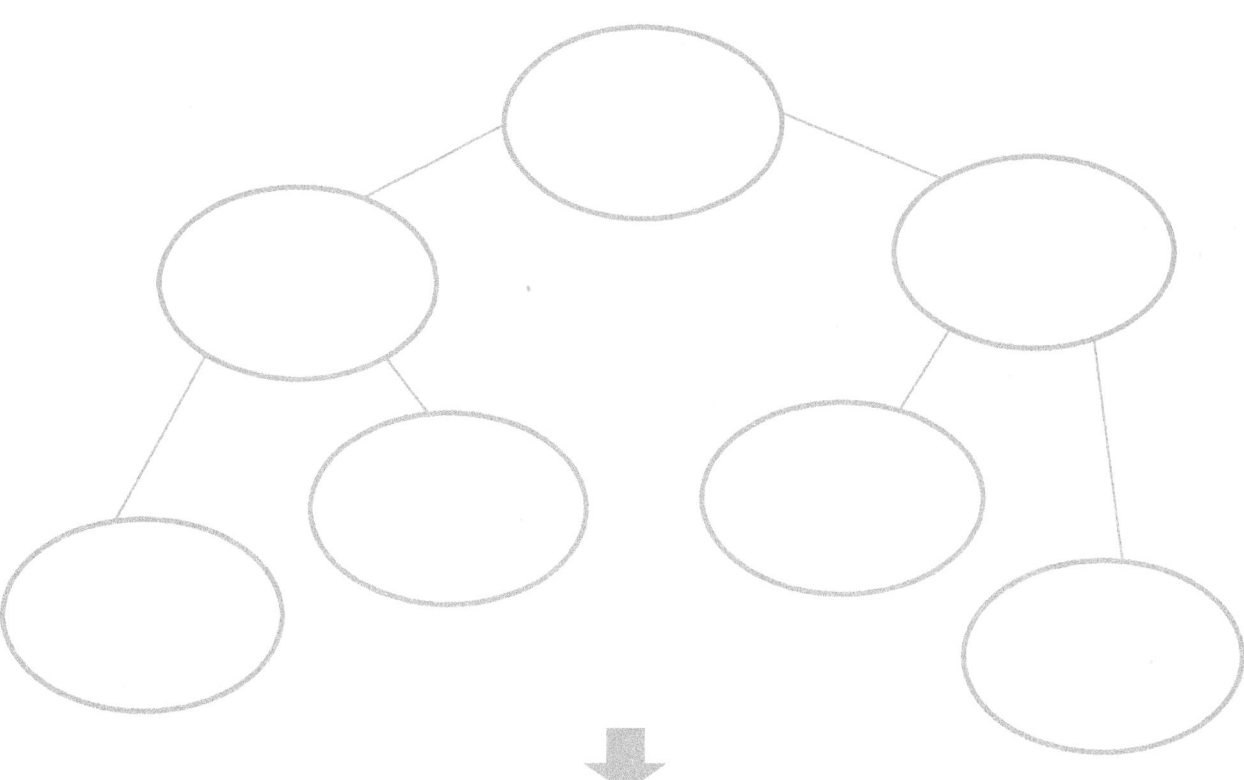

Brainstorm

> **Thesis**
> The company should support (**the environment** / **the arts**) because _____
> _____.

RESPONSE 30:00 min

_____

The company should support (**the arts** / **the environment**) because _____

_____

First, the business should make a donation to (**the arts** / **the environment**) because _____

_____

_____

Furthermore, the company should make a donation to (**the arts** / **the environment**) because _____

_____

_____

In conclusion, _____

_____

_____

Independent Writing Task

> **Prompt**
> A large company will donate money to either support the arts or protect the environment. Which option do you think that the business should support? Use specific reasons and examples to support your answer.

donate to the arts	donate to the environment
	env. needs more help
	set ex. for other companies

Brainstorm

- support env.
  - needs more help
    - humans harm env.
    - env. necessary for survival
  - set a good ex.
    - others might donate
    - companies → env. friendly

> **Thesis**
> The company should support (*__the environment__* / **the arts**) because *the environment is in urgent need of help, and because doing so might inspire other companies to make donations*.

MODEL ANSWER

Each year, the destruction of natural habitats through development and pollution grows worse. The company should support the environment because the environment is in urgent need of help, and because doing so might inspire other companies to make donations.

First, the business should make a donation to the environment because the environment needs more support than the arts. As our population increases, air pollution harms plants, animals, and people while water pollution affects drinking water. The environment needs this support right away because such pollution threatens our existence.

Furthermore, the company should make a donation to the environment because doing so would set an example for other companies. Many companies damage the environment in order to make their products. Companies need to realize that saving the environment comes before making profits. If one large business starts making donations, others may follow along. In time, all companies might become more environmentally friendly and decrease industrial pollution.

In conclusion, while the arts contribute to people's happiness, the environment is necessary to our survival. Therefore, the environment needs more support than the arts. The company should donate to the environment and inspire other companies to do so, possibly changing the whole nature of business culture.

Integrated Writing Task

PASSAGE

Standardized Testing

Annual standardized testing for all students is crucial for a balanced education. Standardized testing makes sure that during the school year, teachers are providing their students with the most important skills and information. Moreover, standardized testing is a fair, unbiased measure of a student's gains in learning compared to other students around the state. It is more objective than a grade given by a teacher.

LECTURE

Education today relies too heavily on standardized testing. The tests make teachers focus on test preparation for an entire year rather than on students' opportunities for creativity and self-expression. In addition, multiple-choice tests are unfair and inaccurate ways of assessing how much a student has learned in school. Such tests simply can't examine what a student has actually learned, such as social skills, learning skills, or subject information that doesn't happen to appear on the test.

PASSAGE NOTES

Standardized tests are (**helpful** / **harmful**) to education because they

- _____
  _____
  _____

- _____
  _____
  _____

LECTURE NOTES

Standardized tests are (**helpful** / **harmful**) to education because

- _____
  _____
  _____

- _____
  _____
  _____

RESPONSE

20:00 min

> **Prompt**
> Summarize the points made in the lecture, being sure to explain how they relate to specific points made in the passage.

The lecture discusses _____

_____

The lecture **(supports / refutes)** information presented in the reading passage.

First, the lecture claims that _____

_____

_____

This lecture information **(supports / refutes)** information from the reading passage because the reading maintains that _____

_____

_____

Additionally, the lecture asserts that _____

_____

_____

The lecture **(supports / refutes)** claims made in the passage because the passage states that _____

_____

ACTUAL PRACTICE ♦ CHAPTER 4

Integrated Writing Task

M.I. main idea   D1 detail 1   D2 detail 2

PASSAGE

Standardized Testing

M.I. Annual standardized testing for all students is crucial for a balanced education. **D1** Standardized testing makes sure that during the school year, teachers are providing their students with the most important skills and information. Moreover, **D2** standardized testing is a fair, unbiased measure of a student's gains in learning compared to other students around the state. It is more objective than a grade given by a teacher.

LECTURE

M.I. *Education today relies too heavily on standardized testing.* **D1** *The tests make teachers focus on test preparation for an entire year rather than on students' opportunities for creativity and self-expression. In addition, multiple-choice tests are unfair and inaccurate ways of assessing how much a student has learned in school.* **D2** *Such tests simply can't examine what a student has actually learned, such as social skills, learning skills, or subject information that doesn't happen to appear on the test.*

PASSAGE NOTES

Standardized tests: (*helpful* / harmful) to edu.

- *make sure teachers provide the most important info.*

- *fair & objective*

LECTURE NOTES

Standardized tests: (helpful / *harmful*) to edu.

- *teachers → focus all learning on prep. for the test*

- *not fair*

MODEL ANSWER

  The lecture discusses the harm caused by focusing on standardized test preparation in the classroom. The lecture refutes information presented in the reading passage.

  First, the lecture claims that standardized test preparation prevents teachers from encouraging creativity. This lecture information refutes information from the reading passage because the reading maintains that standardized test preparation gives students a balanced education.

  Additionally, the lecture asserts that multiple choice tests are unfair because these tests cannot examine every aspect of a student's progress. The lecture refutes claims made in the passage because the passage states that these tests are a fair measure of a student's learning due to the fact that standardized tests are unbiased.

SYNONYM PRACTICE

Using the word bank below, find two synonyms to match each word in the list below. Then write the corresponding synonyms on the lines provided.

1)	insignificant	important	mysterious	essential
2)	fair	neutral	efficient	effective
3)	incorrect	ideal	perfect	flawed
4)	altering	evaluating	determining	change
5)	discuss	state	analyze	study

1) crucial   _____   _____

2) objective   _____   _____

3) inaccurate   _____   _____

4) assessing   _____   _____

5) examine   _____   _____

Independent Writing Task

> **Prompt**
> The government has announced that it plans to build a new university. Some people think that your community would be a good place for a new university. Compare the advantages and disadvantages of establishing a new university in your community. Use specific details in your discussion.

advantages of a new university	disadvantages of a new university
_____	_____
_____	_____

Brainstorm

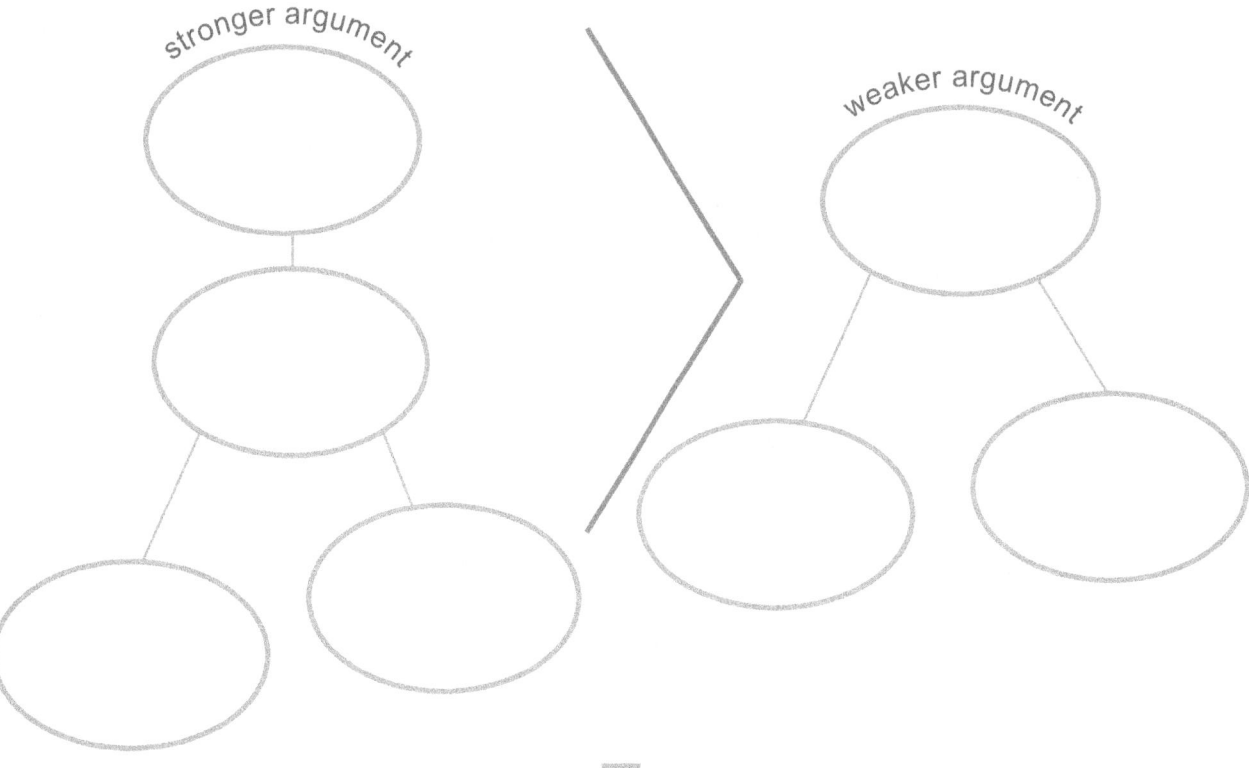

> **Thesis**
> My community (**would** / **would not**) be an ideal location for a new university because _____
> _____.

RESPONSE 30:00 min

_____

_____

My community (**would** / **would not**) be an ideal location for a new university because _____

_____

On the one hand, some people think _____

_____

_____

_____

On the other hand, many believe _____

_____

_____

_____

To conclude, _____

_____

_____

_____

Independent Writing Task

> **Prompt**
> The government has announced that it plans to build a new university. Some people think that your community would be a good place for a new university. Compare the advantages and disadvantages of establishing a new university in your community. Use specific details in your discussion.

advantages of a new university	disadvantages of a new university
bring honor	not enough space
attract smart ppl.	↑ pollution, use of roads, parks

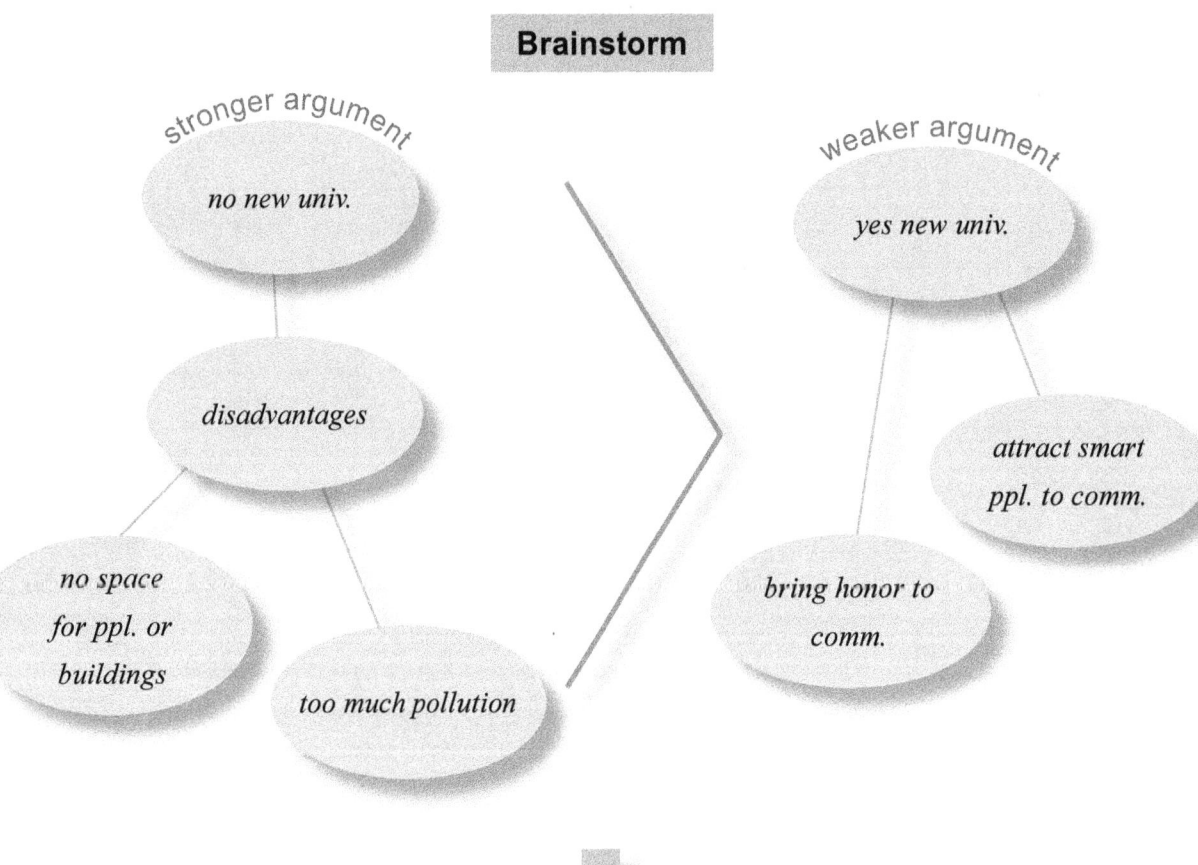

▸ **Thesis** ◂

My community (**would** / **_would not_**) be an ideal place for a new university because <u>a large university may overcrowd and pollute the area</u>.

MODEL ANSWER

The construction of a new university is a major project, and one must carefully consider the advantages and disadvantages that it may bring to a community. My community would not be an ideal place for a new university because a large university will overcrowd and pollute the area.

On the one hand, some people in my community would welcome a university because it is a status symbol. A university would draw many educated instructors and graduate students to the area. It would also bring bright students who might remain in the community after they graduated.

On the other hand, I believe that my community is a bad place for a new university because there is not enough space to contain a large university. Currently, there are about 10,000 residents in my town. The university would bring thousands of students and employees, essentially doubling the size of the town. This population increase would generate development and pollution, which would damage my community's character.

To conclude, while some people may want to build a university in my community, the disadvantages outweigh the advantages. My community is too small to support a university. Ultimately, the government should build the university elsewhere.

Integrated Writing Task

PASSAGE

Eleanor Roosevelt

Respected throughout the world, Eleanor Roosevelt was the wife of Franklin D. Roosevelt, president of the United States from 1933 to 1945. By becoming involved in national social reforms and humanitarian efforts, Eleanor Roosevelt provided a strong female voice in American politics. Furthermore, Mrs. Roosevelt also influenced international politics. She became a representative for the United Nations on behalf of the U.S. shortly after serving as first lady.

LECTURE

As the reading states, Eleanor Roosevelt had a huge impact on issues in both domestic and international politics. In addition to being a powerful female role model, she also contributed to the International Congress of Working Women, where she addressed issues related to gender and poverty. Moreover, during her time with the United Nations, she helped write the Universal Declaration of Human Rights, which establishes fundamental rights for all people, regardless of nationality.

PASSAGE NOTES

Eleanor Roosevelt was a (**positive** / **negative**) influence.

She was involved in

- _____
_____
_____

- _____
_____
_____

LECTURE NOTES

Eleanor Roosevelt was a (**positive** / **negative**) influence.

She was involved in

- _____
_____
_____

- _____
_____
_____

RESPONSE

20:00 min

> **Prompt**
> Summarize the points made in the lecture, being sure to explain how they relate to specific points made in the passage.

The lecture discusses _____

_____

The lecture **(supports / refutes)** information presented in the reading passage.

For one, the lecture states that _____

_____

_____

This lecture information **(supports / refutes)** information from the reading passage, which states that _____

_____

_____

Additionally, the lecture asserts that _____

_____

_____

The lecture **(supports / refutes)** claims made in the passage because the passage emphasizes _____

_____

ACTUAL PRACTICE ♦ CHAPTER 4

Integrated Writing Task

M.I. main idea   D1 detail 1   D2 detail 2

PASSAGE

Eleanor Roosevelt

M.I. Respected throughout the world, Eleanor Roosevelt was the wife of Franklin D. Roosevelt, president of the United States from 1933 to 1945. **D1** By becoming involved in national social reforms and humanitarian efforts, Eleanor Roosevelt provided a strong female voice in American politics. **D2** Furthermore, Mrs. Roosevelt also influenced international politics. She became a representative for the United Nations on behalf of the U.S. shortly after serving as first lady.

LECTURE

M.I. As the reading states, Eleanor Roosevelt had a huge impact on issues in both domestic and international politics. **D1** In addition to being a powerful female role model, she also contributed to the International Congress of Working Women, where she addressed issues related to gender and poverty. **D2** Moreover, during her time with the United Nations, she helped write the Universal Declaration of Human Rights, which establishes fundamental rights for all people, regardless of nationality.

PASSAGE NOTES

Eleanor Roosevelt was a (**positive** / negative) influence.

She was involved in

- *soc. reforms & human. efforts*
- *U.N. rep.*

LECTURE NOTES

Eleanor Roosevelt was a (**positive** / negative) influence.

She was involved in

- *Int'l Cong. of Working Women (gender, poverty); female role model*
- *in U.N. → helped w/ Univ. Dec. of Human Rights (for all ppl.)*

MODEL ANSWER

      The lecture discusses the political contributions of First Lady Eleanor Roosevelt. The lecture supports information presented in the reading passage.

      For one, the lecture states that Mrs. Roosevelt helped bring attention to issues such as poverty and women's rights by participating in the International Congress of Working Women. This lecture information supports information from the reading passage, which states that Eleanor Roosevelt was a positive female role model in politics.

      Additionally, the lecture asserts that Eleanor Roosevelt spent her time in the United Nations establishing basic rights for people from every nation. The lecture supports claims made in the passage because the passage emphasizes Mrs. Roosevelt's international influence, such as her joining the U.N. right after serving as first lady of the United States.

SYNONYM PRACTICE

Using the word bank below, find two synonyms to match each word in the list below. Then write the corresponding synonyms on the lines provided.

1)	rejected	admired	appreciated	ignored
2)	accepted	included	affected	changed
3)	thoughtful	strong	influential	demanding
4)	concerns	problems	answers	solutions
5)	sets	denies	founds	rejects

1) respected   _____   _____

2) influenced   _____   _____

3) powerful   _____   _____

4) issues   _____   _____

5) establishes   _____   _____

Independent Writing Task

> **Prompt**
> In general, people are living longer now. Discuss the causes of this phenomenon. Use specific reasons and details to develop your essay.

Notes

People live longer today because

1) _____

2) _____

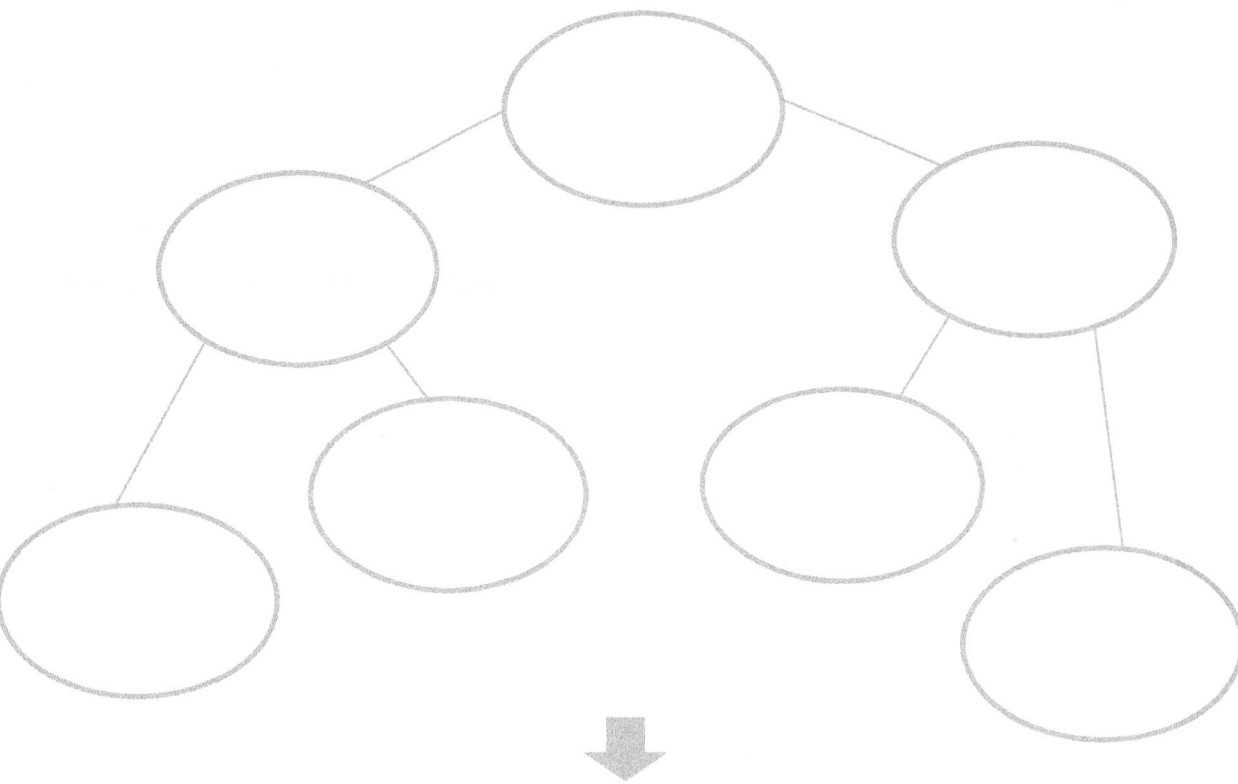

▸ **Thesis** ◂

People live longer today because _____

_____.

RESPONSE 30:00 min

People live longer today because _____

First, _____

Second, _____

To conclude, _____

Independent Writing Task

> **Prompt**
> In general, people are living longer now. Discuss the causes of this phenomenon. Use specific reasons and details to develop your essay.

Notes

People live longer today because

1) *improvements in medicine*

2) *production of healthy foods*

Brainstorm

- better medicine & nutrition
  - medicine
    - ↓ disease severity
    - vaccines ↓ many diseases
  - healthy foods
    - easier to avoid, fight diseases
    - tech → adequate food

> **Thesis**

People live longer today because *of improvements in medicine and food production.*

MODEL ANSWER

Current data indicates that people worldwide are living longer than previous generations. People live longer today for a number of reasons, including improvements in medicine and food production.

First, people are living longer due to improvements in medicine. Only a couple of centuries ago, diseases such as smallpox and tuberculosis threatened millions of lives every year. However, research in the 19th and 20th centuries has led to the development of vaccines that have eliminated many diseases. Furthermore, antibiotics, heart monitors, and many other medical innovations have helped extend life expectancy in modern society.

Second, food security has helped many people avoid getting diseases and has increased the chances of survival even if they become ill. Although many people in the world still experience a lack of adequate food, for the industrialized world the problem has become too much food. The technologies to grow, refrigerate, process, and store food have on the whole contributed to better nutrition globally.

To conclude, a number of factors such as improvements in medicine and improved production of food have increased the number of years that people are expected to live. As society advances, we find new ways to extend life by improving our overall health.

TOEFL PATTERN WRITING 1

Chapter 5

ACTUAL TEST

Integrated Writing Task

PASSAGE

The Ancient Greek Poet Homer

The Greek poet Homer is traditionally identified as the author of the epic poems the *Iliad* and the *Odyssey*. Many scholars believe that he was from the Ionian Islands because the language of his poems matches the Greek dialect used there. He probably lived sometime between 800 and 700 BCE, as many events described in Homer's epics accurately describe the social, political, and economic conditions of Greece at that time, although his stories were set in even more ancient times. Furthermore, many Greek writers in later centuries spoke of Homer as a real, historical figure. For instance, the historian Herodotus, who lived in the 5th century BCE, believed that Homer had lived 400 years before him.

LECTURE

Currently, not everyone agrees that there really was a poet named "Homer." Many scholars believe that over generations, many people retold and expanded the scenes in the *Iliad* and the *Odyssey*. Moreover, there's no proof of an individual Homer. The dialect in which the poems were written tells us nothing about the poems' origins, only about the person who decided to write them down. Secondly, although the poems seem to describe a particular century, that doesn't indicate a single composer; storytellers everywhere change details in stories to fit their own time. Finally, Herodotus and other ancient Greeks who wrote about Homer's life were describing events that occurred centuries earlier. By that time, the poet Homer was already a mythic figure.

RESPONSE

20:00 min

> **Prompt**
> Summarize the points made in the lecture, being sure to explain how they relate to specific points made in the passage.

ACTUAL TEST

Independent Writing Task

Prompt
If you could study a subject that you never had the opportunity to study, what would you choose? Explain your choice, using specific reasons and details.

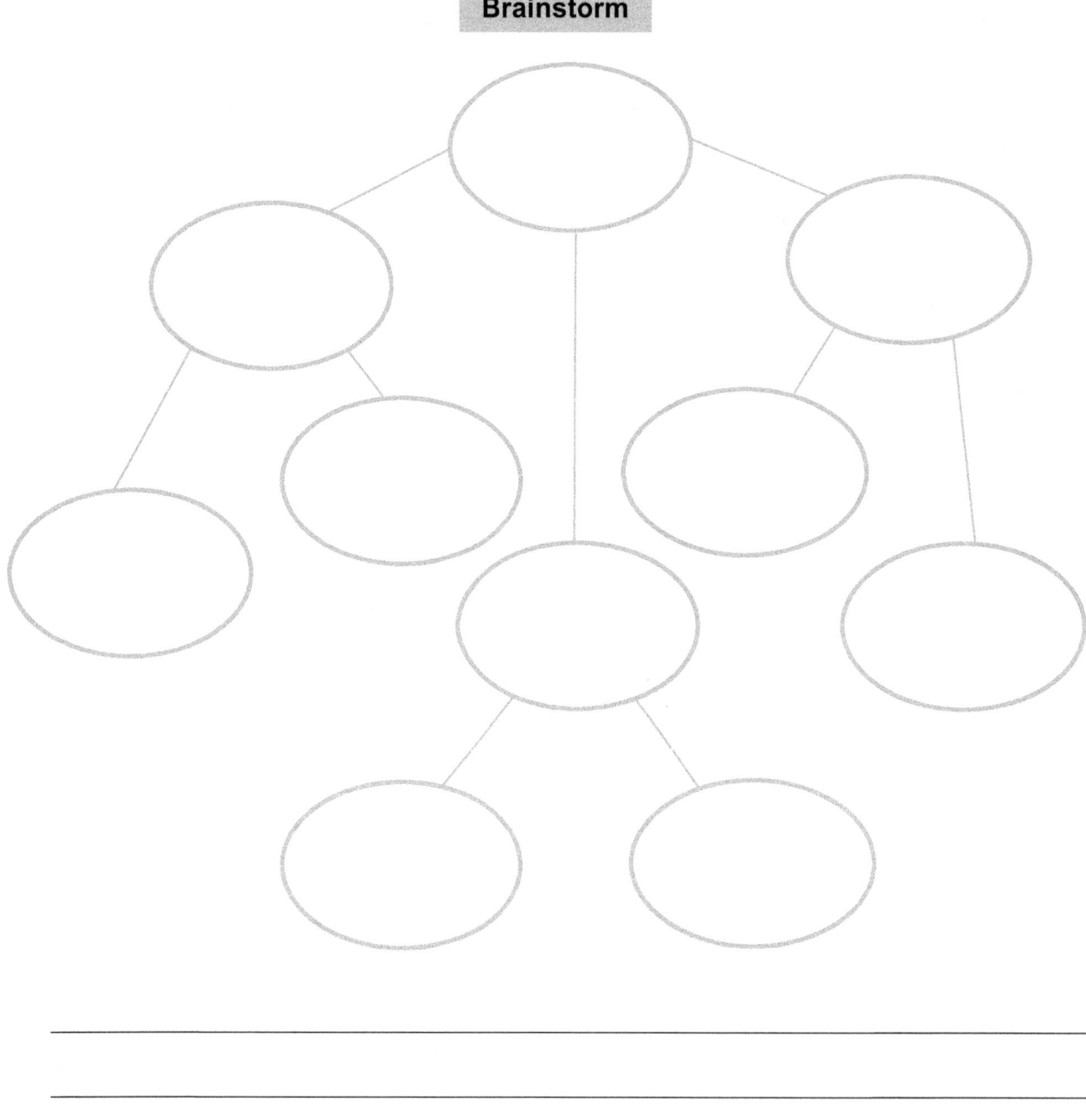

RESPONSE 30:00 min

Integrated Writing Task

M.I. main idea   D1 detail 1   D2 detail 2

PASSAGE

The Ancient Greek Poet Homer

M.I. The Greek poet Homer is traditionally identified as the author of the epic poems the *Iliad* and the *Odyssey*. Many scholars believe that **D1** he was from the Ionian Islands because the language of his poems matches the Greek dialect used there. **D2** He probably lived sometime between 800 and 700 BCE, as many events described in Homer's epics accurately describe the social, political, and economic conditions of Greece at that time, although his stories were set in even more ancient times. Furthermore, **D3** many Greek writers in later centuries spoke of Homer as a real historical figure. For instance, the historian Herodotus, who lived in the 5th century BCE, believed that Homer had lived 400 years before him.

LECTURE

M.I. Currently, not everyone agrees that there really was a poet named "Homer." Many scholars believe that over generations, many people retold and expanded the scenes in the Iliad and the Odyssey. Moreover, there's no proof of an individual Homer. **D1** The dialect in which the poems were written tells us nothing about the poems' origins, only about the person who decided to write them down. Secondly, **D2** although the poems seem to describe a particular century, that doesn't indicate a single composer; storytellers everywhere change details in stories to fit their own time. Finally, **D3** Herodotus and other ancient Greeks who wrote about Homer's life were describing events that occurred centuries earlier. By that time, the poet Homer was already a mythic figure.

PASSAGE NOTES

traditionally: Homer = author of the epic poems

- *his homeland → Ionian dialect*
- *epics reveal conditions of 800-700 BCE*
- *ancient writers refer to Homer / real figure*

LECTURE NOTES

Homer real person?

poems expanded / many people?

- *dialect doesn't prove origin*
- *any storytellers → change poems to fit times*
- *ancient writers uninformed / myths only*

MODEL ANSWER

> **Prompt**
> Summarize the points made in the lecture, being sure to explain how they relate to specific points made in the passage.

The lecture questions the existence of the Greek poet Homer, who supposedly wrote the *Iliad* and the *Odyssey*. The lecture refutes the points made in the reading passage.

For one, the lecture claims that the Greek dialect used in the poems does not tell us where the poems originated, as someone else could have written the stories down long after they were first told. This refutes the passage's claim that Homer likely came from the Ionian Islands, as the language of the poems matches the Ionian dialect.

Moreover, the lecture asserts that different poets over many years could have changed the events in the poems to match social and political situations that were occurring during their own lives. This point refutes the claim made in the passage that Homer must have lived at a certain time because the poems reflect the conditions of that era.

Finally, the lecture states that ancient historians, such as Herodotus, knew nothing but myths about Homer, making their claims unreliable. This statement refutes the passage, which claims that Homer must have been an actual person because ancient writers assumed he was.

ACTUAL TEST

Independent Writing Task

> **Prompt**
> If you could study a subject that you never had the opportunity to study, what would you choose? Explain your choice, using specific reasons and details.

Brainstorm

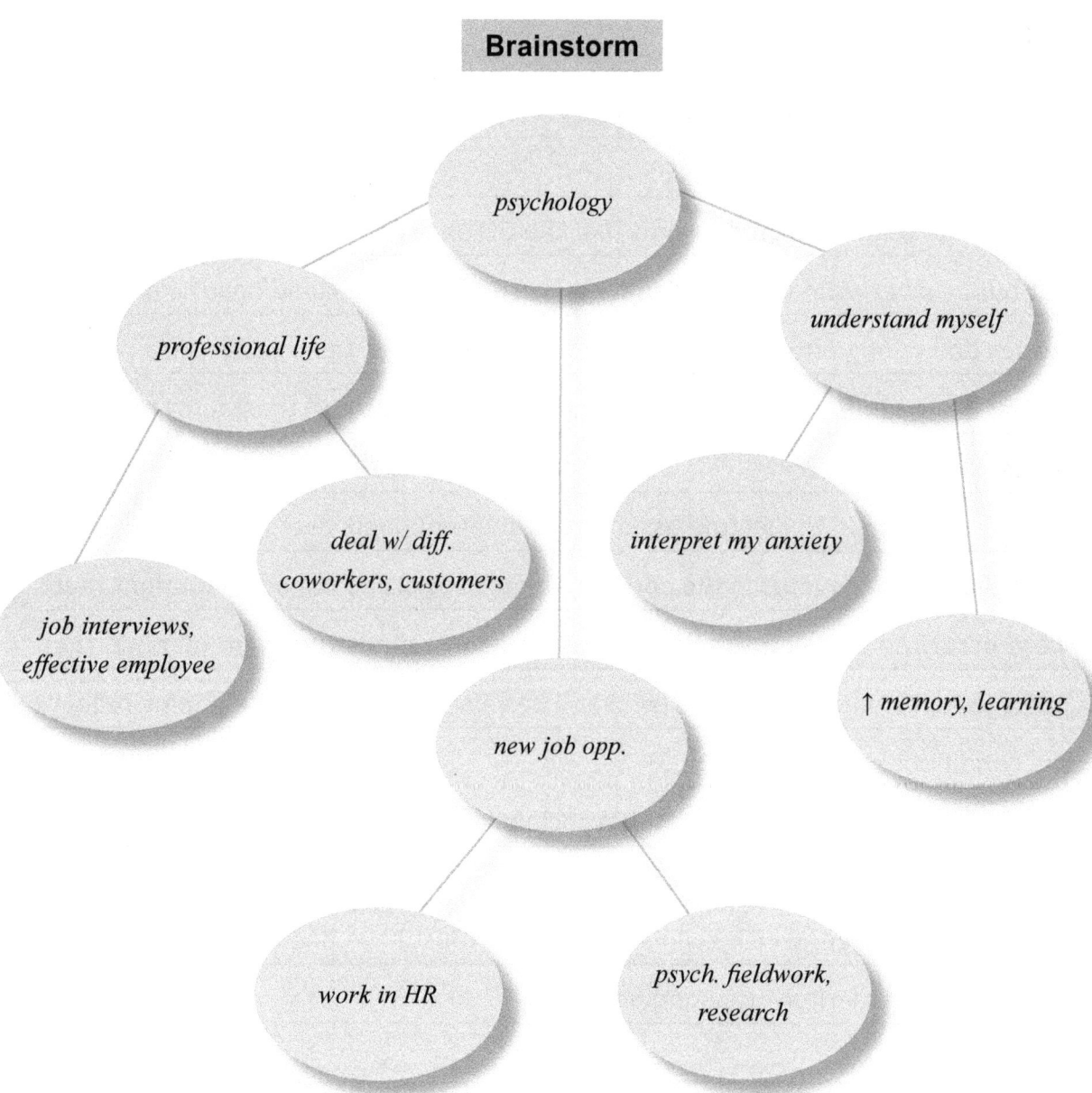

MODEL ANSWER

Studying any unfamiliar subject would likely improve my life. Given the opportunity, I would study psychology because it would be of great help in my professional and personal life.

First, studying psychology would help me interact with others in my professional life. For example, business psychology classes would help me interview for jobs and be a more efficient employee. Likewise, classes in areas such as behavioral psychology would help me deal with difficult coworkers or customers. If I could understand why challenging people act a certain way, maybe I could better understand how to get along with them.

Second, psychology could potentially lead to exciting new job opportunities. On the one hand, perhaps I could use my newfound understanding of human behavior to work in an office setting in human resources. On the other hand, I could pursue psychology related fieldwork as a professional researcher; this career would allow me to contribute meaningful knowledge to the field. Thus, pursuing psychology would open up new and interesting careers.

Finally, psychology could help me understand myself. For example, I tend to be a very anxious person. Classes in areas such as neurobiology and clinical psychology may help me understand why I become anxious and help me learn to manage my condition. Likewise, I would like to improve my ability to learn and remember information, and classes in cognitive psychology may offer insight into that process.

Psychology would help me understand myself and others, so I would definitely take the opportunity to study it. I doubt that any other subject could offer me so many benefits.

Appendix

ANSWER KEY

TOEFL PATTERN WRITING 1

Answers may vary on many of the Practices; the answers provided are samples, and they are not the only acceptable responses.

CHAPTER 1

SKILL 1

p. 3
PRACTICE 1
2) The statement seems correct.
3) The researcher did many experiments.
4) Many people celebrate holidays with their families.
5) The student spent many months on her research project.
6) Journalists present the facts to readers.

PRACTICE 2
3) F   4) F   5) S   6) S
7) S   8) F   9) F   10) S

PRACTICE 3 (*Answers will vary.*)
1) An important day of the year *in America is Independence Day.*
2) My home country *has a population of about 300 million people.*

p. 4
PRACTICE 1
2) Holidays are great times to visit friends.
3) During the winter, it is easy for people to spread illnesses to other people.
4) Sick people should stay home to avoid spreading germs.
5) Parents enjoy playing video games with their children.

p. 5
PRACTICE 2
2) The lecture disputes the claim that **computers** will completely replace **humans** in **workplaces**.
3) **People** often rely on the support of **family members** during **difficult times**.
4) Reading **newspaper articles** and watching **news programs** can help **people** stay informed about **current events**.
5) **Small countries** may require **young people** to serve as **soldiers**, which may provide **them** with **valuable life experiences**.
6) **Children** who **excel** in **sports** may receive **college scholarships**, or **they** may even receive **offers** from **professional sports teams**.
7) **Firefighters** must be willing to place **themselves** in **dangerous situations**, such as entering **burning buildings** or putting out **forest fires**.
8) **Cellular phones** that can access the Internet **are** the best **gifts** that **parents** can give to **their children** because **cellular phones** provide access to useful information.

p. 7
PRACTICE 1
2) The/A, an   3) a, the
4) The, the   5) an, a
6) The, the   7) The, the

PRACTICE 2
2) **The** final exam was so easy that it only took **the** students **an** hour to finish.
3) **The** elephant at **the** zoo is **the** largest animal that I have ever seen in person.
4) In **the** year 1969, Neil Armstrong became **the** first man to walk on **the** Moon.
5) One leg of **the** table was shorter than **the** other legs, so Sam put **a** wedge under it.
6) While at **the** beach, I ate **a** sandwich and watched **the** waves crash into **the** sand.
7) **The** octopus was able to escape its aquarium by squeezing its body through **a** crack in **the** aquarium lid.

p. 9
PRACTICE 1
2) **Many/Most** of the students failed their tests.
3) **A lot of/Plenty of/Much** flour is needed for the recipe.
4) I cannot believe that **so few** of my friends want to see a movie.
5) Some people like to wake up early while **other** people like to sleep in.

PRACTICE 2
2) a couple of   3) a little
4) plenty of   5) most of
6) some

SKILL 2

p. 11
PRACTICE 1
2) Blue whales eat
3) Sperm whales dive
4) Researchers attach
5) Most whales rely
6) Beluga whales make
7) A male humpback whale sings
8) microphones collect

PRACTICE 2
2) am   3) are
4) were   5) will be

p. 13
PRACTICE 1
2) lasts
3) completes
4) encircles
5) increases

PRACTICE 2
2) does   3) denies
4) studies   5) cries
6) undergoes 7) applies
8) tries   9) forgoes
10) does   11) undoes
12) flies

p. 15
PRACTICE 1
2) prepared, will prepare
3) lived, will live
4) spoke, will speak
5) had, will have
6) put, will put

PRACTICE 2

2) gave 3) saw
4) made 5) went
6) chose 7) felt
8) thought 9) knew
10) spoke 11) became

p. 17
PRACTICE 1

2) forgotten, talking
3) walked, becoming
4) malfunctioning, lost
5) practiced, winning
6) passed, studying

PRACTICE 2 (*Answers will vary.*)

1) I am planning to attend a university.
2) I have completed high school.
3) I am planning to go to Switzerland.
4) My friend has quit his job as a waiter.
5) Society is becoming busier.
6) More people have started to shop online.

p. 19
PRACTICE 1

2) Her hard work impressed me.
3) Eventually, she chose a job in the field of health care.
4) Now, my sister helps many people when they get sick.
5) She taught me the importance of having goals.

PRACTICE 2

2) The lost cat climbed a tree.
3) Doctors saved the patient's life.
4) A loud noise scared away the deer.
5) Grandma will appreciate my homemade gift.
6) Psychologists conducted a study to see why people like karaoke.
7) The writer presents evidence that proves his point.

p. 21
PRACTICE 1

2) Ricky made the tutor explain the math problem.
3) The guard let the prisoners out of their cells.
4) Martha helped her son with his homework.
5) Carrie let the doctor look at her broken leg.
6) Richard helped Chelsea move her belongings.

PRACTICE 2

2) Lisa got her essay corrected.
3) Amy had her clothes cleaned.
4) Doug had his car repainted.
5) Joe had his lost wallet returned to him.
6) Francis had his dinner delivered to his house.

SKILL 3

p. 23
PRACTICE 1

2) they 3) his
4) its 5) we, our
6) they, their 7) it, its

PRACTICE 2

2) The last piece of cake is yours.
3) The dog buried its bone in the yard.
4) Help your brother with his homework.
5) My mother told me to prepare dinner.
6) The penguins returned to their nests with food.
7) Sally and I walk to school with our friends every day.

p. 25
PRACTICE 1

2) Peter, **who** lives next door, is very friendly.
3) The house **that** Julie lives in is very old. / The house **where** Julie lives is very old.
4) Diana works in that office building, **which** will be rebuilt soon.
5) The hotel **that** we stayed in was not very clean. / The hotel **where** we stayed was not very clean.
6) Laurence's favorite fruit is kiwi, **which** is the national fruit of China.
7) Grandfather bought this property in 1934, **when** land was very inexpensive.
8) California, **which** is the most populated state, has very diverse geography.

PRACTICE 2

2) that 3) These
4) this 5) that
6) these/those 7) those
8) those

p. 27
PRACTICE 1

2) Anyone can succeed if **he or she** tries hard enough.
3) Honestly, either of the choices **is** fine with me.
4) Both of them **are** excited to move to a larger city.
5) Sometimes, one of the suspects in a legal case **wins his or her** freedom.
6) No one can determine what will happen to **himself or herself** in the future.
7) Each **child** who wants to attend school should have a right to do so.
8) Each of the three boys **is** going to take **his** dog to the park to play for a while.
9) Any student who is interested in studying abroad should send in **his or her** application.
10) No person can avoid making mistakes; in fact, **he or she** will make many mistakes throughout life.
11) It is great to see a student who keeps up with **his or her** schoolwork and exercises in **his or her** free time.

SKILL 4

p. 29
PRACTICE 1

2) longer…than

3) more solitary than
4) more colorful than
5) more aggressive than
6) better than
7) more peaceful than
8) higher than

PRACTICE 2
2) the shyest
3) the loudest
4) the farthest
5) the longest
6) the smartest
7) the most violent
8) the most
9) the most playful

p. 31
PRACTICE 1
2) saving, spending
3) playing, solving
4) reading, speaking
5) sending, finding
6) eating, predicting

PRACTICE 2 (Answers will vary.)
2) …to get enough sleep each night.
3) …to ignore figures of authority.
4) …to become nervous before a test.
5) …to go on a long vacation.
6) …to purchase a new car.
7) …to take responsibility for your own actions.

p. 33
PRACTICE 1
2) Fears can go away. Some people report **feeling** better when they practice **facing** their fears bit by bit. For example, a person who fears heights can practice **going** up a small ladder.
3) Fears can grow worse over time. Doctors suggest **confronting** what one fears. For example, if one fears open places, he or she should not stop **going** outside.

PRACTICE 2
2) to investigate   3) to see

4) to answer   5) to go
6) to send   7) to end
8) to talk

p. 35
PRACTICE 1
1) materials, belongings
2) suitable, pleasant
3) typically, ordinarily, routinely
4) many, an abundance, numerous
5) disagreeable, awful, harmful
6) type, variety, sort

PRACTICE 2
2) broken down   3) came across
4) as long as   5) cut back on
6) give up   7) find out
8) so far

p. 37
PRACTICE 1
2) is   3) are
4) goes   5) collects
6) has   7) states

PRACTICE 2
2) In college, I studied literature, physics, and math.
3) My grandfather enjoys reading, walking, and sleeping.
4) A good friend should be honest, trustworthy, and kind.
5) A successful basketball player should be able to pass, dribble, and shoot the ball.
6) Ron will receive a promotion because he is very smart, he works hard, and he is never late.
7) Choosing the right university can be difficult, but choosing the right profession is even harder.

p. 38
PRACTICE

I am	it is	is not
I will	it will	was not
I have	it would	are not
I would	we are	were not
you are	we will	do not

you will	we have	does not
you have	we would	did not
you would	they are	cannot
he is/has	they will	could not
he will	they have	will not
he would	they would	would not
she is/has	there is/has	have not
she will	there are	has not
she would	there will	had not

p. 39
PRACTICE 1
2) I am going to travel for a while after college.
3) He did not want to run for president again.
4) Do not touch the dog when it is eating, or it is going to bite you.
5) The writer probably does not want to point out the drawbacks of the plan.
6) It is always going to be helpful to review topics that you have learned in school.

PRACTICE 2
There are special aspects to every time of year, but my favorite season is fall. I have two main reasons for loving fall. One is that after a dry, hot summer, the cool air and rain are a relief, and I just want to be outdoors. Secondly, during fall, my family starts planning what we are going to do for the winter holidays. It is always an exciting time, even though we have to start a new school year.

p. 41
PRACTICE 1 (Answers will vary.)
2) I usually brush my teeth in the morning.
3) I socialize with my friends at a coffee shop.
4) I usually wake up at 8:00 a.m. in the morning.
5) I might go to a bookstore to relax on my own.

PRACTICE 2

2) Having chosen teams, the boys begin to play soccer.
3) Writing in red ink, the teacher made many corrections.

SKILL 5

p. 43

PRACTICE 1

2) Egyptians covered a body in special salt for weeks, **so** it would dry out.
3) They added wine, spices, oil, wax, and gum, **and** then they wrapped the body in cloth.
4) Before 2000 BCE, Egyptians placed mummies in a wooden box, **but** later they began using an inner and outer box.
5) They painted an illustration of the person's face on the box, **and** the painted faces were often lifelike.
6) They might paint the rest of the box with scenes of gods, **or** they might paint symbols.

PRACTICE 2

2) After
3) While
4) Although
5) if
6) because

p. 45

PRACTICE 1

2) Cd: Ants are small, **but/yet** they are highly efficient workers.
   Cx: **Although** they are small, ants are highly efficient workers.
3) Cd: We can go watch a movie, **or** we can go eat dinner.
   Cx: **While** we can go watch a movie, we can also go eat dinner.
4) Cd: I will make dinner for myself, **for** I am hungry.
   Cx: I will make dinner for myself **because** I am hungry.
5) Cd: Kelly is always late for school, **so** she received detention.
   Cx: **Because** Kelly is always late for school, she received detention.
6) Cd: Janet forgot her wallet at home, **so** her friend paid for her dinner.
   Cx: **Because** Janet forgot her wallet at home, her friend paid for her dinner.
7) Cd: Mark rushed to the supermarket, **but/yet** it closed before he arrived there.
   Cx: **Although** Mark rushed to the supermarket, it closed before he arrived there.
8) Cd: Charles studied for his final exam, **so** he received an "A" on the test.
   Cx: **Because** Charles studied for his final exam, he received an "A" on the test.

p. 47

PRACTICE 1

2) According to
3) For instance
4) However

PRACTICE 2

1) Afterward
2) Thus
3) Nevertheless
4) For example

CHAPTER 2

SKILL 2

p. 54

PRACTICE 1 (*Answers will vary.*)

1) • 1970 → 3.5 bil. ppl.
   • 2013 → 7 bil. ppl.
2) • Columbus → Caribbean in 1492
   • wanted route to Asia
3) • E. Native Am. home = wigwam
   • wigwam = wooden, dome-shape
4) • Dec. 1903 → Wright bros. flight
   • Wright Flyer = first flight
5) • ecosystem = animal & env. relationship
   • can be large or small
6) • old belief: gods → game outcomes
   • coin/dice used in impt. decisions
7) • 1850: CA → state
   • gold found → pop. ↑
8) • dystopia = bad future setting
   • often show current soc. issues
9) • learn. helpless. = can't solve issues
   • ex: student fails → stops studying
10) • autobio. = writing abt. own life
    • term: 18th c., concept much older

p. 57

PRACTICE 1

2) The lecture **refutes** the passage.
3) The lecture **supports** the passage.
4) The lecture **refutes** the passage.
5) The lecture **supports** the passage.
6) The lecture **supports** the passage.

p. 59

PRACTICE 1

2) According to the passage, fossils are used "to understand extinct plants and animals."
3) b. For example, found, studying
   c. determined, certain, unlike
4) According to the author, scientists used fossil evidence to determine that birds are the direct descendants of some dinosaur species.

p. 60

PRACTICE 2

1) The passage claims that Arnold "is often considered one of the greatest traitors in American history."
2) According to the passage, "Arnold became a top leader in America's Continental Army in 1775," during the onset of the American Revolution.
3) a. bravery, significant, repeatedly
   b. thought, unfair, incapable

c. effort, give up, was unsuccessful
4) According to the author, Benedict Arnold betrayed America during the American Revolution because Arnold felt he was being treated unfairly by unjust American leaders.

p. 61
PRACTICE 3
1) The author states, "Isaac Newton published his most influential book, the *Principia*," in 1687.
2) The passage claims that the *Principia* "laid the foundation for research in mathematics and physics."
3) a. explains, states, hits
   b. includes, correctly, effect
   c. Furthermore, create, foundation
4) According to the author, the ideas stated in Newton's *Principia* have had a huge impact on modern mathematics and sciences.

SKILL 3
p. 63
PRACTICE 1 (*Answers will vary.*)
2) the causes of the decline of the Mayan civilization; refutes
3) 19th-century African-American female authors; supports
4) the effects of raising the minimum wage; refutes

p. 65
PRACTICE 1 (*Answers will vary.*)
2) The lecture claims that sports arenas create overcrowded roadways, which have economic drawbacks. This lecture information refutes information from the reading passage because the passage states that constructing a sports arena benefits a community financially.
3) The lecture asserts that most Vikings were not vicious or violent. These claims refute the passage, which maintains that Vikings used more frightening weapons than others.

SKILL 4
p. 75
PRACTICE 1 (*Answers will vary.*)
The lecture **discusses** the benefits of storing toxic materials underground. The lecture **disagrees with** the passage, which talks about the disadvantages of underground toxic waste storage.

First, the lecture states that underground storage keeps toxic **waste** safe from environmental conditions. This information differs from claims in the reading passage, **which** state that toxic waste storage can lead to groundwater contamination.

CHAPTER 3

SKILL 2
p. 84
PRACTICE 1 (*Answers will vary.*)
1) One positive trend in my generation is that people are starting to show more concern about the impact of human activities on the environment.
2) A holiday custom that I value in my culture is sharing a meal with my family during Thanksgiving, because doing so allows me to share stories and fond memories with them.
3) During summer in my community, many people enjoy going to the beach, as the weather is warm and sunny during the summer months.
4) I would rather have a quiet coworker because I am more productive when I can work in peaceful, quiet conditions.
5) I think that the most important quality for a good roommate to have is calmness because I become anxious when those around me are chaotic or dramatic.
6) Sometimes, it is more fun to visit a new place with a companion because it is always better to share new experiences.
7) It is beneficial for me to have a job right now because I need the money to pay for my tuition.
8) Loyalty is a more important quality in a friend than honesty because a friend that is too honest about everything might end up hurting my feelings.
9) The most important characteristic of an excellent teacher is the ability to inspire students because people learn more when they are interested in what is being taught.
10) My perspective on jobs and careers comes from my past experiences, such as seeing how committed my parents were to their jobs.

p. 87
PRACTICE 1
see p. 86 for a sample timeline

SKILL 3
p. 90
PRACTICE 2 (*Answers will vary.*)
agree
• best weather
• no school

♦ **Brainstorm**
agree
• *best weather*
  • *outdoor activities (surf, bike)*
  • *long, warm days*
• *no school*
  • *time for vacation*
  • *spend time w/ friends*

disagree
• fall → better weather
• winter → most exciting holidays

◆ **Brainstorm**

disagree
- *fall → better weather*
  - *cooler weather*
  - *scenery (trees) more beautiful*
- *winter → most exciting holidays*
  - *Christmas Day*
  - *New Year's Day*

p. 91
PRACTICE 3 (Answers will vary.)
hot climate better
- more time outside
- less $ on clothes

cold climate better
- fun winter activities

◆ **Brainstorm**

hot climate better
- *↑ time outside*
  - *tan/relax outside*
  - *activities (bike, run)*
- *less $ on clothes*
  - *need less layers of clothes*
  - *warm weather clothes cost less*

cold climate
- *fun winter activities*
  - *sledding, snowboarding*
  - *stay inside, board games*

p. 92
PRACTICE 4 (Answers will vary.)
The most important academic subject is *literature*.

Reasons:
- ↑ vocab.
- challenge viewpoints

◆ **Brainstorm**

lit. most impt.
- *↑ vocab.*
  - *help socially*
  - *help in job/career*
- *challenge viewpts.*
  - *become more accepting*
  - *change own opinions*

p. 93
PRACTICE 5 (Answers will vary.)
agree
- social skills impt.
- friends → for life

◆ **Brainstorm**

agree
- *social skills impt.*
  - *job interviews*
  - *making new friends*
- *friends → life*
  - *learn life lessons from them*
  - *rely on them in hard times*

disagree
- grades impt.
- lead to success

◆ **Brainstorm**

disagree
- *grades impt.*
  - *get into univ.*
  - *impress peers*
- *lead to success*
  - *↑ job opp.*
  - *care for fam. ↑*

p. 96
PRACTICE 1 (Answers will vary.)
2)
agree
- always have friends
- someone to ask for help

◆ **General Statement**

There are times in every person's life when he or she needs support, compassion, or just someone to listen to a problem.

◆ **Thesis**

I believe that having a sibling is better than being an only child because siblings can provide support and companionship.

disagree
- learn independence
- receive ↑ parental attention

◆ **General Statement**

Although there are many benefits to growing up in a big family with many brothers and sisters, being raised as an only child can be quite beneficial, too.

◆ **Thesis**

I believe that having siblings is not better than being an only child because being an only child teaches you how to be independent, yet you still receive plenty of parental attention.

3)
agree
- classes → common interests
- lots of time around same ppl.

◆ **General Statement**

Although the primary purpose of attending school is to focus on academic achievement, it also provides young people with important opportunities to meet like-minded individuals.

◆ **Thesis**

In my opinion, the best place to make new friends is at school because fellow students have similar classes to discuss, and it is possible to get to know them over long periods of time.

disagree
- focus on studies
- clubs → common interests

◆ **General Statement**

School provides children with opportunities to learn about hard work, dedication, and academics, so school is not a place to socialize with friends.

◆ **Thesis**

In my opinion, the best place to make new friends is not at school because during school, children should focus on their studies, while extracurricular activities provide better opportunities for finding friendship.

4)
agree
- complete homework
- study for tests

◆ **General Statement**
Many would argue that the stress of meeting project deadlines and attending long meetings for one's job is more difficult than succeeding in school.

◆ **Thesis**
I think that doing well in school does require more effort than maintaining a career because a student must deal with completing homework and studying for tests.

disagree
- project deadlines
- meetings

◆ **General Statement**
Many people claim that the stress of completing homework assignments and taking tests is more difficult than successfully maintaining a career.

◆ **Thesis**
I think that doing well in school does not require more effort than maintaining a career because an employee must deal with the pressure of meeting project deadlines and attending long conferences.

p. 98

PRACTICE 2 (Answers will vary.)
2)
agree
- support self
- save $

◆ **General Statement**
Some people believe that attending college is necessary in order to discover one's passion and find a good job.

◆ **Thesis**
In my opinion, getting a job right after high school is preferable to attending a university because doing so allows a person to be independent and to save money for the future.

disagree
- good job after college
- discover your passion

◆ **General Statement**
Many people will argue that earning money and gaining work experience by getting a job right after high school is a wise decision.

◆ **Thesis**
In my opinion, getting a job right after high school is not preferable to attending a university because a university education provides time to discover one's interests and provides better job opportunities later in life.

3)
traveling alone
- flexible schedule
- meet new ppl.

◆ **General Statement**
As is shown by the popularity of tour groups, many people like to travel with others because it gives them the opportunity to bond with their fellow travelers.

◆ **Thesis**
Personally, I prefer to travel alone because doing so allows me to have a more flexible travel schedule and to meet new people.

traveling with others
- time to bond
- ↓ boredom

◆ **General Statement**
People travel for many reasons: to visit family, to immerse themselves in another culture, or to experience the beauty of nature. And all these experiences are better when shared with a traveling companion.

◆ **Thesis**
Personally, I prefer to travel with others because doing so gives me time to bond with my traveling companions and ensures that I will not get lonely or bored.

4)
working while in school
- save $ for univ.
- meet new ppl.

◆ **General Statement**
Many people argue that not working while attending school gives them more time to study and socialize.

◆ **Thesis**
Personally, I believe that working while attending school is preferable because doing so allows me to save money to pay for university fees and meet new people at my place of work.

not working while in school
- ↑ time to study
- ↑ time to socialize

◆ **General Statement**
Many people claim working and attending a university at the same time has many benefits, such as being able to save money and meet new people.

◆ **Thesis**
Personally, I believe that not working while attending school is preferable because doing so gives me more time to study and more opportunities to socialize.

p. 100

PRACTICE 3 (Answers will vary.)
2) My favorite place to visit on vaca-

tion is *Hawaii*.

Reasons:
- tropical weather
- forests, volcanos, & beaches to explore

♦ **General Statement**

Should an ideal vacation location be filled with new and exciting places to explore? Or should it be filled with sunny, relaxing beaches? Fortunately, when a person visits Hawaii, they don't have to decide.

♦ **Thesis**

My favorite place to visit on vacation is Hawaii because this chain of islands features tropical weather, unique forests and volcanos, and beautiful beaches.

3) **Motivations**:
- passionate abt. certain field
- exp. a place diff. from home

♦ **General Statement**

Although many people want to go to a university so they can spend all their time socializing, there are also many productive, life-changing reasons to pursue a university education.

♦ **Thesis**

I believe that a person might want to study at a university because they want to become an expert in a field that they are passionate about, or they may want to experience an environment that is different from their hometown.

4) **The best place to spend time with friends is** *a coffee shop*.

Reasons:
- can get coffee drinks
- comfortable chairs/couches

♦ **General Statement**

Many people like to spend time with their friends in the comfort of their own homes, where they can talk and watch television together.

♦ **Thesis**

In my opinion, the best place to socialize is a coffee shop because one can relax in comfort while enjoying coffee drinks.

SKILL 4

p. 103

PRACTICE 1 (*Answers will vary.*)

2) Exp. 1: Fast and effective search engines allow Internet users to access almost any piece of information in just seconds.
   Exp. 2: Social media, such as Facebook and Twitter, gives people separated by great distances an easy way to communicate.

3) Exp. 1: The library is always quiet, so it is easy to focus for long periods of time.
   Exp. 2: The library has thousands of books as well as Internet access, making it the best place to research for a test or writing assignment.

4) Exp. 1: Newspaper articles cover a large variety of topics, such as politics, arts, and sports.
   Exp. 2: Newspaper articles generally provide more in-depth analysis than do television news programs.

5) Exp. 1: Swimming does not put as much stress on one's joints and bones as running does.
   Exp. 2: Swimming exercises almost every muscle group in the body, something that few other exercises can accomplish.

6) Exp. 1: A large, healthy breakfast gives me the energy I need to be productive throughout the day.
   Exp. 2: Breakfast foods, such as eggs and waffles, are easy to cook, and they taste delicious.

7) Exp. 1: Watching the news on television keeps a person up-to-date on current events both locally and internationally.
   Exp. 2: Watching documentaries can present useful, interesting information in an engaging way.

8) Exp. 1: Earning good grades will show a student that hard work results in success, which boosts self-confidence.
   Exp. 2: Achieving academic success will often result in praise from others, which lets the student know that others are impressed by his or her hard work.

9) Exp. 1: People will respect a leader who demonstrates that he or she cares for the welfare of others.
   Exp. 2: A compassionate ruler will take the wants and needs of others into consideration when making decisions.

10) Exp. 1: The process of creating a major would encourage students to be both organized and imaginative.
    Exp. 2: Students who can pursue exactly what they are interested in will work harder, leading to better grades and enthusiastic students.

p. 105

PRACTICE 1 (*Answers will vary.*)

Topic Sentence 1

Exp. 2: Speaking confidently during a job interview will show a potential employer that one is confident and comfortable in social situations.

Topic Sentence 2

Exp. 1: When meeting a person for

the first time, being able to speak clearly will make one seem confident and friendly.

Exp. 2: Public speaking experience helps a person stay calm and engaging during discussions with friends.

Topic Sentence 3

Exp. 1: Having public speaking skills helps one to organize and express thoughts, which is a valuable skill when writing.

Exp. 2: Public speaking requires one to analyze arguments, question others' opinions, and develop critical thinking skills.

p. 107

PRACTICE 1 (*Answers will vary.*)

2) In conclusion, many people enjoy reading or relaxing at home after a stressful day. However, in my opinion, nothing gets rid of stress better than exercises such as running and swimming. After a long work out, all my anxiety has gone away, and I feel alert and ready to move onto the next big challenge.

3) Overall, it is important for children to develop strong communication skills. Because learning a new language requires children to develop these skills, all children should be required to learn a foreign language in school. By doing so from a young age, children will grow up with much more compassion and become more understanding toward others.

SKILL 5

p. 113

PRACTICE 1 (*Answers will vary.*)

One place that I have always wanted to visit is New York City. I want to visit this city because it contains so many interesting neighborhoods and cultural attractions.

For one, I want to visit New York City because I would like to see the Statue of Liberty. It is one of the most recognizable symbols of the United States. Although I have seen many photographs of the enormous statue, I would like to see it in person.

Thus, of all the places in the world that I could visit, New York City would be the most exciting.

CHAPTER 4

p. 121

SYNONYM PRACTICE 1

2) aid, help
3) useless, unsuccessful
4) help, support
5) main, major

p. 129

SYNONYM PRACTICE 2

1) found, uncovered
2) proof, clue
3) huge, large
4) belief, idea
5) discuss, state

p. 137

SYNONYM PRACTICE 3

1) important, essential
2) fair, neutral
3) incorrect, flawed
4) evaluating, determining
5) analyze, study

p. 145

SYNONYM PRACTICE 4

1) admired, appreciated
2) affected, changed
3) strong, influential
4) concerns, problems
5) sets, founds